The Weight of Ghosts

The Weight of Ghosts

*on love and loss
and motherhood and writing*

LAILA HALABY

Red Hen Press | *Pasadena, CA*

Book layout by Mark E. Cull

Library of Congress Cataloging-in-Publication Data

Names: Halaby, Laila, author.
Title: The weight of ghosts: on love and loss and motherhood and writing /
    Laila Halaby.
Description: Pasadena, CA: Red Hen Press, 2023.
Identifiers: LCCN 2023020792 (print) | LCCN 2023020793 (ebook) | ISBN
    9781636281346 (paperback) | ISBN 9781636281353 (ebook)
Subjects: LCSH: Halaby, Laila. | Women authors, American—Biography. |
    Mothers—United States—Biography. | Women immigrants—United
    States—Biography. | Parental grief—United States. | Mothers and
    sons—United States.
Classification: LCC PS3608.A5455 Z46 2023 (print) | LCC PS3608.A5455
    (ebook) | DDC 813/.6 [B]—dc23/eng/20230531
LC record available at https://lccn.loc.gov/2023020792
LC ebook record available at https://lccn.loc.gov/2023020793

The National Endowment for the Arts, the Los Angeles County Arts Com-
mission, the Ahmanson Foundation, the Dwight Stuart Youth Fund, the Max
Factor Family Foundation, the Pasadena Tournament of Roses Foundation,
the Pasadena Arts & Culture Commission and the City of Pasadena Cultural
Affairs Division, the City of Los Angeles Department of Cultural Affairs, the
Audrey & Sydney Irmas Charitable Foundation, the Meta & George Rosenberg
Foundation, the Albert and Elaine Borchard Foundation, the Adams Family
Foundation, Amazon Literary Partnership, the Sam Francis Foundation, and
the Mara W. Breech Foundation partially support Red Hen Press.

First Edition
Published by Red Hen Press
www.redhen.org

a reminder:

your story
is your story

and a dedication:

to the mums

and to the sons
with us in all forms

The Weight of Ghosts

there was or there wasn't

My older son, Raad, drove west on I-10 shortly after two o'clock on a rainy February morning.

The hours leading up to those moments had not been eventful. He was recovering from a cold and had slept late and done errands. He had eaten leftover Chinese food for dinner and read at the dining room table. He left our house before nine to meet a friend for drinks at the Kingfisher, a bar that no longer exists. Toward the end of the evening he or his friend called a girl he had been seeing. There was a misunderstanding and the bar was loud and she hung up. He and his friend left the bar sometime after one.

Someone came home briefly. Turned on lights, made noise. Turned off lights, closed the door.

At some point Raad got on the highway heading west. He was probably listening to country music. Sturgill Simpson, perhaps.

He had just crossed into Pinal County when, for reasons unknown, he pulled onto the left shoulder and got out of his truck.

At 2:35 a 911 call was made by the codriver of the eighteen-wheeler that had hit and killed him. Three subsequent calls were made by drivers who had tried to avoid hitting what they thought was debris in the road.

"We don't know what happened. In 99 percent of the cases, I can tell you exactly what was going on with each of the drivers involved to get them to where they were. In the case of your son, we just don't know. He is that 1 percent."

"I am so sorry for your loss; I can't imagine what you are going through."

"God has a reason, even if you can't see it."

"I saw him in my side mirror with his hands in the air."

"He got his ambiguous movie ending."

"There is no making sense of this; just accepting."

"You need to live for the living."

"You are going to have to come up with a story about what happened that makes sense to you and just hold onto that."

"Maybe God was protecting him from something worse."

"You are going to have to deal with some shit to get through this."

"Nothing is ever going to be the same."

"You may need to reinvent yourself."

"Go live somewhere else."

"The only way through it is through it."

Part One

All the things about ourselves that we think are so terrible—to other people, it's just a bit more information about us.

—Derren Brown

Let's be clear about what motherhood is. A being comes onto this earth and you are charged with keeping it alive. It dies if you do not tend it. It is as simple as that. No matter how intellectual and multicolored motherhood becomes as children grow older, the part that says *My purpose on earth is to keep you alive* has never totally dissipated. Magical thinking on all sides.

—Elizabeth Alexander

Chapter One

I was never given the rights to my story and now I am in my fifties like a child starting out in the world, learning my borders, where one self/idea/place ends and another begins.

Writing my story has always felt like a lie; in fiction I can be honest.

For years I have listened to women and men pour out details of mental breaks and trauma and relationship catastrophes, drug addictions, loss, grief, struggle, illness, and abuse. They've talked about wanting to be good parents, good children, good people, and just to be okay. I have held their hands, worn their dresses, carried their backpacks, combed through their knotted hair. I have lifted up the corners of their stories so they could walk a little lighter.

For years I have listened.

My own story made sense in the shadow of theirs.

Tell your story, echo their voices. *Tell your truth.*

I do not tell my truth because to do so would hurt others.

This is America! It's an old-world story! No one cares!

I do not tell my truth because to do so would bring shame to members of my family.

This is life! Things happen! You are not your story!

My mother is eighty-six. Her oldest friend, someone she's known since she was a child, does not know the truth about her former employer or about my father.

You are going to have to look at everything with brutal honesty.

I cannot be honest about who I am without hurting someone.

How to speak freely when my public is private? By making my private public?

My oldest half-brother, who is in his seventies, and the only one on my father's side of the family who knows that I am one of them, will not acknowledge my existence publicly as long as his mother is alive.

I am a fiction.

My story has never been mine to tell. It is squished between other people's tall tales, glopped onto their secrets and lies and mistakes and bad decisions that are interwoven and rib the top and bottom of the place where I currently find myself.

I learned my beginning-story in increments, a crumb here, a corner there. I was in my midtwenties before I was given what I thought was the last bite.

I have written a thousand and one versions of that story in fiction, but I have never said in writing that I am the _____ daughter of _____, former ____ employee, and _____, _____, deceased.

I am not ready.

❦

I am mixed. 50.7 percent Western Asian/North African, 49.3 percent Northern European. 100 percent illegitimate. Unacceptable on both sides of the Atlantic. I am almost perfectly balanced in my own *chueca* way. I am a seesaw that only ever gets stuck up or down if someone else climbs on. I can find easy motion or quiet stillness, my long Western Asian/North African/Northern European legs dangling evenly in the air.

My white mother taught me that I had to know who I was, what I came from, and that I had to be proud of that.

She also lied about who my father was and what she did for a living and insisted that I was Caucasian.

I hadn't understood that she could do two very opposite things at the same time: encourage me to be confident in who and what I am while filling my head with the myth of white privilege and superiority.

My body rejected this spoon-feeding—both versions—and I got very good at spitting.

The white man who loved me for several years said that he knew I was the one for him the day we went for a picnic and I spat cherry pits down a hill. Thhhuup. They'd fly out of my mouth and land several feet away. He was prone to exaggeration and the more he told this story, the greater the distance of my spitting.

By the end I could spit for miles.

He, The White Man I Loved (TWMIL), who had grown up on a farm in the South and thought my story was wonderful, told me I was too literal; prior to him saying that, I thought I was a really honest person, a pride I carried because I was born of lies.

My mother was trained as a lawyer. She will argue the other side of any topic just for the sake of it.

Being mixed, I can see both sides to almost any story and sometimes struggle to know which one to choose.

Being a bastard, it can take me a while to stand up for myself, though I get there eventually, usually with an attitude of righteousness.

Weeks after Raad's accident, when I was still raw and broken and on good days I could open the curtains—this was before I started taking medication that would numb me to fear and feelings—TWMIL grew frustrated by my inertia and told me that he needed a partner, someone who would go with him when he went, for instance, into the desert to cut branches for the wood-burning stove he had purchased from a man in a forest. While I could not get her to come out, the me-I-once-was lay deep inside her darkened room giggling and asking if we lived on a homestead in the 1800s. The me-I-had-become stood numb and silent in front of his house—the one he had given me the key to after three weeks of knowing—in the dirt driveway, under the blazing sun, and said goodbye to him as he left for the desert with his chainsaw.

He needed me to trust him that I would feel better if I went with him to chop wood/play volleyball/have a beer/go hiking/do anything.

"You are stuck," he'd tell me.

"I am grieving," I'd respond.

My younger son was in and out of rehab. Then in and out of drama.

During the beginning months when my younger son was away,

I couldn't bear to be in my house and I stayed with TWMIL. At first, I needed space and quiet.

"The back room is yours," he told me. "Use it for writing or whatever you need. If you're in there I will leave you alone." He did.

He went on trips in the world while I roamed around his house and took baths and talked to birds.

And then I needed purpose and meaningful engagement.

He gave me tasks to do on a house he was remodeling. He planned trips for us.

I saw friends and accepted jobs without telling him.

After months and months and months that added to more than a year of me pushing him away but not having the courage to do more, we parted.

"I can't do this," he told me. "My mind is all over the place and I am working with dangerous equipment."

"I can't be the person you want me to be," I told him for the hundredth time.

We had an agreed-upon separation but missed each other's company and we unparted.

Nothing had changed. I was still turtle-paced when I walked with him through Home Depot or crying in bars with my back to the world, and he still wanted to go camping and buy a house and have adventures. We both loved each other and we both wanted and valued different things.

He was mostly kind, but his frustration was growing.

"Couples are supposed to live together," he said to me after I had fully moved back into my house. "This is supposed to bring us closer."

"Children aren't supposed to die," I replied. "Supposed-tos aren't real."

"If you want to continue with this relationship," he said on a different day, "you are going to have to put out."

Was I really expecting him to be nice and patient indefinitely while I dragged myself from one surface to another and then accepted one job after another?

He needed me to trust him.

He needed me.

His tiny splattering of frustrated words turned into a flood that crept across the floor and stained my feet, seeped up the hem of my jeans. Until then, there had been no escape hatch, only the stone walls of his adoring. That man who loved me didn't want to be moored in a depression harbor any longer. He wanted the me he had fallen in love with to come back and join him on adventures and to have sex with him. Mostly he wanted to feel my love.

My emotions were busy. My love was locked up somewhere.

A few months after I had met him, I had written, "Girl, you let a white man snag you and now you gonna replay that same stupid story. Careful. You got more important things to take care of, even if he do love you."

My true place was in words and unattainable homelands and in the tiny hyphen I kept erasing, not by the side of a white boyfriend.

Arab Americans had quirky fathers and talked about food.

Palestinians had lost their home but were tied to it.

I was Jordanian American with a Syrian name that matched the queen's.

Writing saved my life.

"You are so emotional," my mother would say.

"You don't have any of the white side in how you see the world," my younger son told me.

"You can totally pass for white," my older son said.

When I was younger, I would tell my story so that others could understand it, not how it actually was.

In other words, I lied to tell the truth.

When people asked why my parents divorced, I said it was due to complicated family issues, which is only a lie if you take into account that my parents were never married, a fact I did not possess until I was twelve.

When I was living in Irbid, I said I was engaged because it made things easier for me to write and work and go about my days without unnecessary hassle and explanation.

I even wore a ring.

A man's non-present presence was my ticket to stability and to being taken seriously.

On the weekends I would visit my father but had to refer to him as my uncle.

When I came back to the States, I said he was dead.

"That's fucked up," my younger son said to me recently.

"It was after a year of him lying about who I was and taking me places where people assumed that I was his girlfriend."

"That is also fucked up."

When I got married and had children, I thought I was done with all of that. I packed my details into a tiny top cabinet that required a ladder to reach. The mess stayed put, the doors stayed shut.

Or so I thought.

The reality was that my details would not be ignored and had begun to seep out almost immediately, dribbling down in quiet rivulets behind walls, rotting floorboards, and corroding pipes. From time to time, I'd notice a squeaky step or a funky smell but was distracted by family and life and a post-9/11 world and the wars in Iraq and divorce and by the killings of Black people and the many-year saga and near tragedy of my younger son and then the actual tragedy of my older son.

Raad dying proved too much for that teeny-tiny cabinet and it vomited its rotted contents across all the floors of my house. You can't step into one room without tripping over Brown or White or Black or Non-White or some kind of struggle battling some kind of privilege, some kind of lie tripping some kind of secret.

I need to put on my house shoes for the duration of this writing.

A few months after I met TWMIL, I T-boned a black Corvette that turned left in front of me as I was driving north on Tucson Boulevard. The second or two before impact, as I pressed my foot deep on the brake, the world went completely silent. And then the airbags went off and I sat, stunned. My once jaunty blue SUV—the only car I had ever bought new—was in the right turn lane and wouldn't start. I got out and walked to the sidewalk, dazed.

He had his hands in the air.

A woman came up to me and said she had seen everything, that the driver of the black Corvette—she pointed to where he had pulled over—was not in a turning lane, had been reckless, and that she would wait for the cops to tell them.

A middle-aged white policeman walked up to me a few minutes later. "Is this your vehicle?" he asked, pointing.

I nodded.

"You need to get it out of the road." he said. He did not ask if I was okay.

"It wouldn't start," I told him. "Airbags went off."

"It's city law that you need to remove your vehicle from the road." He headed back to the young Asian driver of the black Corvette.

I stared at him. Clenched my lips tight against the *fuck you* that was forming.

Firefighters pulled up and moved my car.

I called TWMIL who said he would head over.

After some time, the policeman came back and asked for my license, registration, and insurance, which I handed to him.

"Your insurance is expired."

"It's not. I must have forgotten to switch the card. I've had the same insurance for years, same policy number, you can check."

"We don't check," he said looking at me with tensed muscles in the lower part of his face. "If you can't produce a current card, you will be cited for failure to carry proof of insurance. And that guy," he gestured toward the Corvette and let out a noise that was a mix between disgusted throat clearing and a humph, "is driving on a suspended license." He walked away again.

Some minutes later TWMIL strode toward me, tall and confident, through the parking lot. He was fit, and while he was dressed in cargo shorts and a T-shirt like nearly every other white man in the city, he had a neat haircut and sported his government-issue Oakley sunglasses that cemented his military look.

This time when the policeman came back, he smiled. He greeted

TWMIL and said to me, "Take your time on the insurance. You can usually call them and then show me on your phone."

He smiled again at TWMIL, who said, "Thank you, sir."

And just like that, I had been offered legitimacy.

Chapter Two

Raad was born at 6:13 a.m. on December 19, 1995 at UCLA Hospital in Westwood. He tried to be born five weeks earlier, which would have landed him eight weeks prior to his official—and much more apt—due date, January 6, 1996, Día de los Reyes. The Epiphany.

I had been doing my counseling internship and finishing my fieldwork when I began to have preterm labor and was put on bedrest. I was given medication for contractions that I recorded in a spiral notebook my then-husband had used for computer figurings and that also contained some of his caricatures, goofy blob-people with outsized parts waving or smiling. While he was at work, I marked the times of my contractions in between reading all of Elizabeth George's mysteries and trying not to worry. If the contractions got closer than every seven minutes for more than a certain number of times, I took a pill to calm them. For five weeks, I lay on the various surfaces of our one-bedroom apartment on Keystone Avenue as my belly tightened and relaxed, tightened and relaxed, tightened and relaxed.

My doctor assured me that I would be fine. She was funny and brilliant and my trips to her office were always pleasant and put me at ease. She had a red Corvette that she drove whenever she needed to get to the hospital quickly.

A day or two before I was allowed to get up and move around, my husband came home from work and we drove to Home Depot. I lay in the backseat of our gray Honda Civic that he had parked in a distant corner of the parking lot, and he vanished into the darkening afternoon. When he reappeared two hours later, he was carrying an enormous Christmas tree, larger than any tree I had ever had as a child. He must have tied it to the roof. I think he said they gave it to him for free when he told them his pregnant wife was in the car, but I may have added that detail to my memory. When we brought it into our apartment, it was so tall that the tip scraped the popcorn ceiling.

Shortly after the arrival of the tree, I was released from bedrest and began to go into real labor. When my water broke, we went to the hospital, but they sent us home after a few hours and said it would be quite a while before the baby came. We drove down an unusually peaceful Westwood Boulevard, gentle lights glimmering off the darkened, wet streets, and stopped to get California wraps. I don't remember eating anything, but I have a vague memory of vomiting. And then we were back at the hospital in a room with gray-green walls and I was screaming, too dilated to be medicated. I had not internalized any techniques from those Lamaze classes we took.

Raad arrived, tiny and dark and covered in gunk, alive and screaming with all his toes and fingers and heartbeats and breathing and reflexes intact. My husband, tearful and smiling, cut the umbilical cord and cradled him in his hands.

We came home but had to return to the hospital a day or two later because our perfect baby was yellowish with elevated bilirubin. Since we had already been released, instead of returning to the maternity ward, we were sent to the NICU. Our roommate was a boy who had been born with his heart outside of his chest—something I didn't know was possible to happen—and would die within the year.

During those few days in hospital, I was told by a resident to stop breastfeeding because "the baby has to be under the lights at all times." I told her that I would breastfeed him and put him back. She told me I was doing everything wrong by taking him out and breastfeeding. We went back and forth. The doctor in charge came in and mentioned to my husband that I was overly upset, said something about hormones. My husband said something to the doctor about mothers knowing best.

I continued to breastfeed.

We spent Christmas in the hospital.

And then everything was fine and we went home with our perfect baby.

I spent days folded on top of days soaking him in. I stared at him while he slept, rejoiced in him while he was awake, smiling with him and touching his butter-soft skin. I was in a giddy daze of joy and exhaustion. Mostly I couldn't believe that I had brought this wonderment into the world.

Because that was it, wasn't it?

All those years I had thought I was a mistake, wrong and flawed, *ghalta*, and yet I had somehow managed to bring magic into the world.

I carry the weight of your absence all throughout my minutes, but then get distracted by a friend or a movie and I'm floating in lightness, and then I might find myself pouring a bowl of cereal at ten at night and I see the box of Trader Joe's Honey Nut Cheerios that I still buy because you liked them and I sprinkle some on my own late night snack because it makes me feel like we are eating together; in that split second when I first see the box of cereal and think I will pour you a bowl and we will sit in front of the TV—some gritty European cop show that you've found for me—or just chat and debrief, in that sliver of a second when I think things are still as I wish them to be, I can breathe.

Chapter Three

When my grandmother visited Beirut shortly after my arrival on the scene had derailed my mother's life of intrigue and adventure, she purchased a gold leaf necklace that she would later keep in the top drawer of her dresser, that I would try on with her permission, and that would find its way to me after she died. That necklace was proof that I was not a fiction and was the first of my superhero accessories.

My mother had traveled a great deal in her youth, including several visits to Europe, a flight to the Soviet Union in her midtwenties that she had told no one about, and a trip around the world that consisted of a couple of plane rides and two freighter trips, each with only a handful of other passengers. When she visited Egypt on a separate trip, she fell in love with the warmth of the Arab world; it was just a matter of time before she made her way back. Several years before my birth, my mother moved 5,800 miles away so that she could live a life that made sense to her, settling herself into Amman where she *worked for the State Department* and had a cook and a horse; on weekends she'd skip off to Jerusalem in her convertible MG.

When her pregnancy—seven months along—was discovered by her employer, she was sent back to the States to be officially fired from the government job she had held for years. Still in love with my father and unable to bear the US, she flew to Beirut and gave birth to me there, completely alone.

My father visited and my mother took pictures of him staring off into the distance and also holding me. These are the square black-and-white photos she would keep in her cardboard box of important papers, the ones I would feel guilty about asking to look at when I was a child, the ones that would fill me with shame, the ones that would carry the face of my firstborn son.

My mother flew home to her parents when the aloneness became too much. At my grandfather's insistence, she changed our names so that it would appear she had been married, an effort at legitimacy that made me a tiny bit more impossible. She would not tell me that she had done this thing until I was almost twenty, which meant I referenced a father who did not exist and spent decades having to explain how I was Jordanian with a name that said I was from Aleppo.

And no, I am not related to the queen.

When living with her parents got to be too much, she moved us to New York City to the top floor of a large, Upper East Side apartment with windows facing in three directions. We went to museums and took walks in Central Park. We each ate at our wooden dining tables, small and large, across from each other. I went to All Souls Nursery School on nearby Lexington Avenue, a school that was founded in 1965 and now costs upwards of twenty-five thousand dollars a year.

We spent all summers with my grandparents at their house near the beach.

One late summer afternoon when I was three or four, my mother, my grandfather, and I got in the car to go feed the ducks. We parked in the grass at the top of a small hill and my mother and I went down by the water's edge while my grandfather sat in the passenger seat of the car with his legs swung out and resting on the ground so he could watch us. I was holding a bag of bread crusts and throwing little pieces to the ducks. Out of nowhere, a swan swept out of the water and hurtled toward us. My mother ran up the tiny hill toward the car. I ran after her. My mother was way ahead of me, got to the car, sat in the driver's seat, and closed the door. My grandfather swung his legs in and closed the door. I remained outside the car with a swan that was taller than I was in close pursuit. My grandfather rolled down the window a few inches. "Throw the bread," he shouted. "Throw the bread."

When I finally decided to see a therapist months after Raad's death, my cousin Alice said, "Tell her the story of the swan and she will understand everything."

We fled the scene again when I was five. My mother never liked the cold and felt depressed whenever the sun wasn't out, so she chose Tucson because of the brightness and how it reminded her of Jordan, even though the only person she knew there was a friend of a friend. She rented a house that we lived in for seven years and then, with help from my grandfather, she bought a house around the corner and has lived there ever since.

Throughout my growing up, my mother frequently referenced our poverty, and yet we spent summers at the seashore, where I was perhaps the first Arab to infiltrate the Cape May Beach Club, though I didn't ever think about that, only that I was the—clearly different—granddaughter of a man with some status and a mother who wore a bikini and could bodysurf better than any man or woman for miles around.

As a teenager during one of those summers, I discovered running. I'd wake up each morning, throw on some clothes, and step barefoot onto New Jersey Avenue. I'd walk the hundred steps or so to Wilmington Avenue where it borders Poverty Beach and make my way to the rock pilings. I like to think I hopped ballerina-like along the giant black rocks slick from ocean spray and harboring rats, but I must have stayed on the street until I reached the section where the rocks were filled in and paved. I would run from jetty to boardwalk to beach until the end of town. And then I'd run back.

I ran every day for more than a quarter of a century with breaks when I was very pregnant, when I had the chicken pox, and after each broken toe. Running was my always companion. She'd clear my head and lift me up. She let me eat as many cookies as I wanted. She evened out my moods. "If I ever lose the ability to run," I'd joke to my sons, "find somewhere else to live."

The fall before I met TWMIL, my right leg began staging a revolt. First the knee that had been creaking for years, then a muscle. Then ankle to hip. And not just pain. Sometimes my leg buckled without warning. Other times I couldn't convince it to lift my foot off the ground.

In a bid toward sanity preservation, I joined a gym. On that first January morning when I went to swim, a gaggle of women was rushing in with yoga mats tucked under their arms or slung over their backs.

"They are rushing to relax," I marveled aloud to the man checking pool chemical levels through rectangular lenses that sat crooked on his face.

He laughed. "You and I," the man—who introduced himself as Nick—said, putting us together in the first conversation we ever had. "You and I have been through enough in our lives to know what matters. Rushing doesn't matter."

It was just after seven and he'd already claimed me.

We both stared at the purple mountains with the sun rising behind them. He gestured back toward the steam coasting off the glassy surface of the pool.

"You are number one today. Enjoy."

I felt a twinge. Swimming made me feel powerful.

In the absence of running, swimming kept me from losing my mind.

I was born under the sign of the fish by the side of the Mediterranean.

As a child I rode the waves of the Atlantic Ocean.

As a teenager I swam in the Red Sea.

As an adult in the Pacific Ocean.

As a lover in the Sea of Cortez.

Now I swim in a pool in Arizona.

There are times when my breath expelled in the water creates a riot of bubbles: the marrying of my spirit with Raad's.

And for a split second there is joy.

On Friday nights during those summers by the Atlantic Ocean, my grandparents would doll themselves up for dinner at the yacht club and insist I do the same. When I was older and could refuse to go, I would help my grandfather get ready, lay out his tie and jacket and help him with his cuff links. I would choose my grandmother's jewelry for her, though she would never wear the Beirut necklace. On the rare occasion when I joined them, I felt horribly out of place.

Some summers, my mother and I would also drive to the Poconos to visit her dear friend Sarah, who was divorced, had two sons a little older than me, and rented a large house with three refrigerators and board games and people always visiting. One night—I might have been six or seven—I went with another visiting family to a festival. The other family had a blond girl around my age who was excited to participate in the barn dancing. I loved dancing and was not yet bothered by how uncoordinated I was. There were hundreds of people milling about, and after some simple dances, the caller announced a dance that would entail starting paired with your partner and then snaking out in two parallel lines that would diverge, weave around the whole festival, and then come together again.

Was he out of his mind? I was supposed to hop through the woods behind a stranger and somehow get back to this girl who was the only person I knew in the whole place?

The music began and we each held our partner's hand and began to skip. At the moment the lines split, when you had to let go of the person's hand and go off into the darkness, instead of skipping off behind the person in front of me, I hopped behind my blond partner. She turned her head and gave me a not-friendly, squinty look. When the lines snaked back—after an awful lot of skipping up and down the dark hills—I jumped back next to her, pleased with myself for having found a solution to being lost forever in the woods.

you are the white rose
  that bloomed in November
the plump strawberry
  upside down and perfect in the street
the fat butterfly
  that skittered in front of me
the dove
  nestled in the cool dirt under your window
you are the ridiculous snub-nose dog
  leading its owner
the surprise creosote bush
  greeting the front yard
you are the mint
  coming back with enormous leaves
you are the idea
  to talk to that horse woman
you are the bubbles
  when I swim
the crispness in the air
  the orange bird
I saw while walking the dog
  you are the fat hummingbird
who came to my window when I was crying
  the other hummingbird
who zipped in front of my face on our walk
  you are the knowing to jump back
when that truck hopped the curb inches away from me

Chapter Four

I arrived several minutes late to my first writing class—I had been hanging out with a man I thought of as my boyfriend (the one who I would catch a couple weeks later having sex with my friend)—and opened the door to thirty faces looking up at me. The teacher asked me my name before I had fully entered the room and I replied, "My name may not be on the list," with a heavy accent I do not have naturally but that used to appear when I got nervous or angry.

For the remainder of the semester, I felt I needed to speak with an accent. I avoided talking as much as possible and did not interact with the other students outside of class.

The teacher was young and kind, though toward the end of the semester he gave us this prompt: "You are coming home one evening. It has been raining. There are police and a crowd of people up ahead. As you get closer you see the area in front of your building is taped off and there is a body lying on the ground covered with a sheet. One foot is sticking out and you recognize the sneaker as belonging to . . ." We were supposed to take it from there, but my heart was busy and made it hard for me to think clearly.

I would never know anyone in that situation, I foolishly tried to convince myself.

Even now it makes my heart beat extra.

What was he wearing that night? Do you remember the brand of jeans or shirt?

I did not speak with an accent in my second writing class. My teacher was older and white and male and engaging in a way I responded to then and shudder at now. (The six writing classes I have taken in my life have all been taught by white men.)

My first short story in my second writing class was about a Palestinian man living in Italy. I had micro-descriptions of him lying in bed smoking, watching a fly, reflecting on what he had just done, which we find out toward the end was blow up a bridge. The story was told from his perspective and contained a lot of adverbs. Most of the students liked it. One girl said that she liked the main character so it made her want to understand how he could do this thing. "I never tried to see it from a terrorist's perspective."

The professor eviscerated my story. He mocked it. He sat at the head of our long table and shredded it in front of my classmates. When he returned his copy to me, it was drowning in red ink.

There were two older students I was friendly with: a man in his forties and a woman in her thirties. Both of them thought he overreacted.

"You hit a nerve," the man said.

"It's a good story," the woman told me.

SO MANY ADVERBS was written in red at the top of my paper.

Ghalta. Illegitimate. No rights.

In biology, adaptation is a change or the process of change by which an organism or species becomes better suited to its environment.

My second story was based on an event a friend had recounted one day in the student union. A group of boys was coming home on a bus from their high school in Ramallah to their village. The bus was stopped by Israeli soldiers at a checkpoint—a daily occurrence—and just as the soldiers were getting off the bus, someone whistled. Nothing dramatic, just a whistle. The soldiers demanded to know who did it. No one fessed up. The soldiers made all the boys get off the bus and detained them there by the side of the road all afternoon. And then they told them to walk home. The story did not contain a single adverb.

Everyone liked it, including my professor.

With that story, my writing moved into another category.

I wanted to get better at telling stories, to improve my craft, but I also wanted to live what I imagined to be a real life. Naguib Mahfouz worked as a civil servant all his life, I liked to point out. I had not—and still haven't—bought into the institution of MFAs as a requisite. Writers have been writing forever, I reasoned. The good ones find a way to rise to the surface.

I did not understand that in addition to instruction, knowledge, and experience, an MFA afforded you connections, time, and a lifelong community.

I did not understand that I was not Naguib Mahfouz.

Zora Neale Hurston died alone in a nursing home and was buried in an unmarked grave for thirteen years.

I recuperated from my story the summer I came back from Jordan in my early twenties, my belly swollen with lies. I closed myself in my mother's house and rested. I read and cleaned up her yard and cooked and ran every day. I got a job at a bookstore. And I took my first poetry class.

Until then, my exposure to poetry was limited to my grandmother's letters that included quotes from Robert Frost and Emily Dickinson, whatever I came across in the *New Yorker*—whose poems rarely made sense and often required a dictionary—and Mahmoud Darwish.

I was nervous and uncomfortable heading into class, but I did not speak with an accent. The professor was from Kentucky and was not much older than I was. He was tall and thin. He wore blazers and wrinkly jeans and his crusted blond hair was slicked back— we would learn that he swam every morning, which explained the hair, but also was one of those delicious paradoxical details: he was a heavy smoker and drinker and did not seem like someone who would seek fitness in a university pool early in the morning before coming in to teach. He talked about baseball and pronounced the word *poem* with one syllable. He approached teaching with a gentle kindness and a surprising amount of structure.

My mother had been teaching ESL for several years and often told me stories that her students—mostly refugees from Vietnam—had shared with her. My first poem was about students sitting in class at their desks while maintenance people worked on the air conditioning. Suddenly there is a loud bang and all the students dive under their desks. It was a short poem with the final line, "with my freedom, I will give you yours." In spite of its cringeworthiness and youthful idealism (I had not yet learned to substitute *privilege* for *freedom*), our teacher liked it, and as happened with the whistle story, I felt myself fall into a different category of student. I was not—like the football player who sat next to me—taking a summer poetry class to make up a credit; I was taking it because I was a writer who wanted to learn the mechanics of poetry.

While I would always return to narrative verse, I enjoyed playing with villanelles and sonnets and odes. I went through a sestina stage. I fell in love with the titles of James Wright poems and appreciated Charles Bukowski's narrative. "Poems are stories for people with very short attention spans," our teacher told us in a statement that would change my approach to writing, teaching me to tighten my narrative and embrace my lyricism. I only vaguely acknowledged that we read very few women poets and even fewer poets of color.

I was still swollen and sometimes—because without a belt it put no pressure on my belly—I wore the green dress that I had bought in Italy a couple of years earlier. The dress was thick, crisp cotton, and had leafy patterns dancing across it. It had side slits and decorative pockets and tiny wooden buttons. I had seen many sophisticated Italian women wearing similar dresses and I felt powerful, lovely, and hopeful whenever I wore it.

The day I had bought the dress, our neighbors from home had been visiting Florence and invited me out to dinner. I had put on my dress and waited for them on the sidewalk outside of my apartment building that was located near the train station. A man greeted me and stood near me on the sidewalk. He said a number, I thought at first an address. He repeated this number and stood a little closer. I had no idea what he was talking about and told him so. He repeated the number. I turned away and tried to ignore him. He became insistent. The number increased. He got closer. In a ground-opening moment I understood that he had mistaken me for one of the trans sex workers who also lived in my building.

"This should have been an immediate indication to you that the dress was ghastly," my mother would later say.

I may have shouted at him.

I may also have felt the tiniest bit of pride at having blended into my environment.

"Why do poets kill themselves?" the football player asked.

I don't remember our teacher's answer, only that it was thoughtful and kind.

"Our teacher would never do that; he's too normal," I said to the football player afterwards in what sounds to me now like an ignorant and judgmental plea.

A few days before our last session, my teacher let me read *Days of Summer Gone*, his manuscript that had just been accepted for publication. I devoured it in a night. It was brilliant, loaded with the nostalgia and stories of his Southern life, each poem paced and gentle.

And he had let me read it!

Just as I carried a quirky pride for having been mistaken for an Italian sex worker, here I had been offered a connection as a colleague, a fellow writer. I had entered the fold.

We are all just looking for love and belonging.

The following summer I ran into the football player in a bar. He told me that our teacher had shot himself a few months earlier.

Later, I would call the head of the department in search of information or closure or connection and he would tell me that "death was threaded throughout his writing," as though we all should have seen it coming, as though I was dense for having missed it.

Later, I would order my teacher's book, now slick and shiny and official.

Later, I would fold all of my poems that I wrote that summer in between my teacher's poems.

Later, I would add the large green index card on which he had scribbled comments regarding my poetry and final project—including the line "there's no doubt in my mind you've got the chops"—in between the pages of his slim, shiny book with the naked woman standing in a shipping container on its cover. He had written on both sides of the green index card and over the years I would read his words again and again and again. It was among the few possessions on my mental list of things that needed to be saved in case of fire.

Later, when my younger son was going through his Troubles, after he had exhausted the electronics and jewelry and cash and DVDs, he would collect books from the living room shelves my mother had built when we first moved into this house, when he was so little that he could tuck himself into one of them, and he would take them to the bookstore I had worked at that summer I had taken the poetry class, and he would sell them.

He would take the shiny book with the photograph of the naked woman in the shipping container on its cover, its slimness puffed with all the papers folded between its pages, including the giant green index card with the terrible handwriting promising that I "have the chops" and he would sell it.

He would claim to have no recollection of any of this.

A day later TWMIL and I would go to the bookstore and recover some of the books he took.

We would not find *Days of Summer Gone* bloated with hope and with death.

Even now my stomach flips at the thought.

Even now I think I will find the slim volume somewhere, that I will realize I had just misplaced it.

Even now I expect you to walk in the kitchen door.

The yellow bird feeder rocks back and forth at a sparrow's kick. Another sparrow flies in, muscles itself inside the squirrel guard. We don't have many squirrels here, which was probably why the feeder was 75 percent off at Target. The sparrows nip and peck, sometimes three to four at a time, then they skip down the trunk and onto the ground to see what's misfired. The feeder rocks with all this activity. I've hung it so close to the trunk that a woodpecker can lean in and nibble out of the yellow dish and doesn't have to navigate the squirrel guard. While most of the birds are sparrows, there is a cardinal couple that visits, along with the occasional finch. The cardinals have trouble with the squirrel guard too and usually eat whatever is on the ground.

My ex-husband and I planted the mesquite tree from which it hangs too close to the house. I don't think either of us realized how giant a mesquite tree could grow. The single-paned windows of what is now my bedroom face south, so I don't mind the splash of dark branches blocking the sun with their funky twists and graceful bends.

"Mama, if I were attached to you forever, I wouldn't mind," you told me when you were seven.

Chapter Five

One night, two years before Raad's death, my younger son did not come home, nor did he call to say where he was. It was not the first time—or even the fifth time—this had happened. He was fifteen and tall and I worried about different things than I had the previous year when he hadn't come home and I had called the police, when his Troubles were beginning and Raad and TWMIL and I had just embarked on what would evolve into years of tracking him down at all hours of day and night and picking him up in varying states of high and in trouble from neighborhoods all over the city.

Early the next morning of that umpteenth broken night, TWMIL suggested we go downtown, get coffee from the hipster place with the brick walls and uncomfortable wooden chairs, and drive around to look for him. At the café, we ran into a couple I knew in high school who were living the sort of life that no longer felt available to me, and when I got in the truck with my four-dollar cup of coffee, I cried.

We drove by the bus depot just as a second ambulance pulled in. Both of us automatically craned to see the body on the ground.

"A bum," TWMIL said.

I was too tired to take issue with his word choice. We sat back, silently scanning the bus bays. After a minute or so, TWMIL drove on. The coffee was the perfect mix of hot and very tasty. The morning was crisp and bright.

We looped around a few blocks and pulled up along a strip of Pennington where there was a camp of unhoused people. I saw a figure in the distance with familiar movements. My heart skipped for a second but then the person's head popped up and I saw he was not my younger son. This lost boy was a bit older—in his late teens or early twenties—also light-skinned brown, with a flop of braids, patterned Hawaiian shirt, basketball shorts that were falling down, mismatched socks (I could always tell whether my younger son was using drugs by whether or not his socks matched) and basketball shoes. He was long and leggy like my younger son, had that pull to his face, charisma mixed with brain explosions. He was doing a pirouette between the parking meters, stretching his arms out wide like my son might have done, and leaning in close like he was telling a secret. He swaggered on down the sidewalk.

TWMIL and I sat mesmerized.

Where are your parents, sweet boy? I wanted to ask. *Are they looking for you too?*

I thought about him for days, long after my own son came home. I thought about the magic he had going on and how carrying magic can be a bigger burden than people realize.

Rock, paper, worry.

You always hear parents say that they would know if their kid started using drugs.

I knew.

What no one ever talks about is what to do next.

And after that.

And after that.

And after that.

And then again after that.

And after that.

And again after that.

In most every other aspect of my life I come to things late, Middle-Eastern-Standard-Time late, party's-almost-over-and-I'm-just-pulling-up, but in this I was on top of it, even before it happened.

And still.

Rock, paper, worry.

Doubt is a termite.

When you have an urban Peter Pan for a son, you wait a little longer to take off your bra in the evening and to settle into your pajamas because you don't know if you might have to answer the door or drive somewhere.

You keep your phone charged.

You measure your smile, only a pinch for your sweet boy whose own smile booms in jelly-bean colors and light.

You can't sit down and read a book, but you can read a page, check your email, get another cup of coffee, sweep the floor, pick up your book, apply for a job, wash your coffee cup, pick up the dirty shirt that's lying on the floor.

You sleep too late and wake too early and go crazy every few days from the simple fact that you don't sleep enough ever.

You second-guess everything, question everything, your own self/selfishness in particular.

You avoid looking at old pictures.

You drink too much but never too too much because you might have to be somewhere or answer the door or deal with something.

You haven't read a book in years except mysteries, which are like crack.

You are often irrational.

The running commentary in your head is highly critical and won't ever shut the fuck up.

You clean your house obsessively because you recognize that it is the only aspect of your life over which you have the tiniest bit of control.

And you never know who might come in and see it.

You have a nice home; he clearly comes from a good family.

Chapter Six

Some days I am sure I have been following a blueprint.

That figure from my first writing class—I had imagined a young man with red high-tops instead of World War I–style lace-up boots—had been lying dead in the rain, waiting, for thirty years to come alive. And then to die again.

Before I had children, I saw *A River Runs Through It*, a movie about two sons—though then when I saw it, I would have thought about them as two brothers—one edgy, the other scholarly. One eventually dies. I was deeply shaken by this movie, carrying that grief solidly long, long Before.

I created a character (in a book that to my knowledge Raad never read) who skateboards into traffic and dies. We never know if it was accidental or intentional, if he was playing chicken, or misjudged things, or had it all planned out. I created his mother and knew her grief as though it had been embroidered in me at birth. And I created another character who dealt with the pain of his childhood by taking drugs.

One hazy afternoon, shortly after I had started dating a white man in law enforcement, I was driving on I-10 to pick up my younger son from the private school we sent him to in an effort to prolong his innocence, his childhood, and our hope.

"I am scared that if I am with this guy something will happen to one of my children," I was telling Houri on the phone.

"Scared like based on something that's happened, or fearful in a more general sense?"

I was driving the first part of the same route Raad would take that night he never came home.

"The second one. Nothing I can put my finger on, just a general fear. There's an undercurrent of wrong."

Perhaps it was because he had a stepson who had died a few years before I met him.

Or maybe I had already started sensing his lies.

Turn back.

There have been many, many warning signs/announcements.

Like that time when my younger son was fifteen, had stayed out all night and called in the early hours of Mother's Day asking for a ride home from way on the other side of town. TWMIL and I retrieved him from a tract house in the desert and then went exploring the skeleton of El Rancho Diablo, which had been a swank guest ranch in the forties and fifties, a set for movies, a scene for moonlight swimmers and mobsters, rumors of murders, and an actual shootout that left three people dead just over a decade ago. Now it is a scraggy, dusty scattering of dilapidated buildings, cracked pools, debris, and palm trees. TWMIL poked around inside a small building while I stood creeped out in a doorway.

I felt a shot go through my back.

A hornet.

Get out.

The brain is wired for stories. It takes information and spins it into a narrative for survival.

And the October afternoon when TWMIL was in a rush to go on one of his many recreational adventures and our sweet bird escaped.

Turn back!

I knew this story more than a decade before it had happened.

I have known it always.

On the Wednesday Before, I wrote down gratitudes and wants: *I am grateful for you and your brother.* I wrote of wanting a life of integrity, one in which I was true to myself. I questioned my relationship with TWMIL.

Later, I was running in our neighborhood and saw three perfect pencils lying in the road near the school; I did not stop to move them. A couple days later when I ran down that street, one of the pencils was crushed and another was chipped.

Had I let this happen by doing nothing?

On the Thursday Before, I walked with TWMIL in the Santa Cruz wash on Tohono O'odham land and I asked the universe for deliverance from this man who I loved deeply but who wanted a life very different from the life I wanted for myself. (*Why did I ask for deliverance and not simply for the courage to break up with him?*) An owl flew over me. Message received.

No Trespassing.

On the Friday Before, I was driving through Phoenix to visit my younger son in rehab and I looked at those oncoming highways and actually had the vivid thought that if a semi hit you (someone) you'd never have a chance; it would be over in a flash. I was listening to Bill Withers' "Lovely Day" and *thinking of you.*

Did I draw the blueprint or was I reading it?

The human brain is wired for stories.

The last time I saw Raad, on the Saturday evening Before, he was happy, relaxed, confident. I had been thinking in those few weeks prior that he was really coming into himself. The last thing he said to me before he left the house was that he loved me.

A few weeks After, my mother, TWMIL, and I walked in that same part of the Santa Cruz wash. We were silent and tearful and we didn't stay long. Just as we were pulling out, an owl flew up and over us and I thought, with flashes of my mother and my younger son in my mind, *please don't take anything more from me.* Just before the main road that would take us back to the highway, we were pulled over by tribal police.

The officer who stood by the driver's side of TWMIL's truck was large and serious. "Do you know why I pulled you over?"

"No, sir," replied TWMIL.

"Someone reported shots being fired in the wash. Do you know anything about that?"

"No, sir. We were just going for a walk."

This time.

"Anything off the paved roads is trespassing," the officer said.

Had I known we had been trespassing?

I turned my face away as we were told we were forbidden to enter the wash but could ask permission from a council if we wanted to return. Even in that moment I imagined going to the council on my own and telling my story, sure they would be understanding once I had erased TWMIL from the equation.

The officer let us go.

We drove in silence as I kept my gaze out the window, a quiet goodbye prayer.

I walked on Native lands and shouldn't have, and revenge was visited on me.

Walking on Native lands allowed me to see a sign of what was to come, what was destined to be, know that the fault was not mine.

All of these things happened with no connection to where I was walking, and I am buying into a magical Native stereotype.

This was the bookend to my car crash: legitimacy revoked.

This was the bookend to my car crash: legitimacy conferred.

On the first Mother's Day After, TWMIL and I drove north through a forest at night. He cautioned me about deer, gave clear instructions on how to look for eyes by the side of the road. I had both hands on the steering wheel and was hyper-focused, my eyes scanning the road and completely unprepared for the owl that swooped out of the sky and torpedoed into the front of the truck. A sacrificial owl as penance for crossed messages.

"Recognize the emotions but don't get too caught on the story," Dr. K told me.

❦

The medical examiner emailed that the alcohol in Raad's system was just over the legal limit, "but it was taken from his liver so it's not an accurate reading. All it tells us is that he had alcohol in his system."

She also told me to make sure that the funeral home displayed his hand as it was in "pretty good shape."

I wanted details that would wrap me in the safety of science, not the horror of what had happened. As if that would change anything.

I drove to the gym and screamed with the windows up.

Is it possible to bruise your vocal cords by screaming for many minutes while driving? Does the force of your scream intensify with the speed of your vehicle?

At the last shady stretch before the parking lot, a dove walked slowly into the road. I didn't slow or stop because it's a bird and they always fly up at the last minute.

He had his hands in the air.

I looked into the rearview mirror and saw a burst of feathers.

I controlled my horror until I parked.

My rage bled through the borders of everything. "It's like a sprinkler that keeps coming back," said Dr. K.

I searched online for martial arts and self-defense classes and found an ad for Israeli street fighting.

I have never gotten into a fight. The closest I have had to a physical altercation was with my younger son when he was using drugs.

D offered classes for twenty dollars each if you committed to three.

I googled her to make sure she wasn't a serial killer or Mossad agent. She was barely out of high school.

We agreed to meet at a local community center where she talked for most of the hour about her gym and the shock effect she had on large men because she was young, tiny, and lethal. "I had to use this on a racist lady who attacked me at the mall," she said and held up a six-inch-long piece of metal as thick as my thumb that was attached to her keychain.

She talked about being adopted by white people.

My first twenty dollars was spent on her story and six minutes of blocking.

The second time we met, I sneaked her and her huge bag of pads and mitts into the conference room at my work. She did not seem as cheery as at our previous meeting.

"I'm going to teach you shin kicks," she said, adding that she conditioned her own shins by kicking metal objects. "You need to kill the nerves."

This did not sound well-adjusted.

"Now with groin kicks, you use your shins, not your ankle or your knee. Straight kick. Here, I'll show you. Don't block me."

She stood next to me and kicked me hard in the thigh. The look on her face was not kindness.

Two days later, I still hurt.

TWMIL and I went to Big 5 and bought punching mitts. He held out his mitted palms and I focused on the UFC logo and punched with all the force I could find.

I have never thought of myself as small, petite, or girlie, but my engagement with those black foam pads was lightweight at best.

"Build up your upper body strength," TWMIL suggested.

Thabet joined our third and final meeting at one of the houses TWMIL was renovating. D told us to close our eyes and pay attention; she was going to mimic a random attack and we were supposed to resist our flight/fright/freeze response. We giggled and whispered accented commentary.

She told us we weren't trying hard enough.

We moved onto sparring. We hit and apologized and giggled, hit and apologized and giggled.

Again, she said that we weren't taking things seriously enough.

I punched Thabet.

"Ow!"

"You are worse than teenagers," D told us, scowling.

She texted me a few days later that her car had broken down and was in the shop. Could I front her the money? I gave her the phone number of an MMA fighter Raad knew whose father sold cars.

She texted me a week later that her sister was really sick and could I send her money.

I stopped responding to her texts.

A force to be reckoned with, TWMIL said.

A storm, my father called me.

You are fearless, my son's therapist told me. *Men don't like fearless.*

You are not fearless, a man with alarms on his house and an aversion to walking outside in the dark said.

Three hummingbirds whiz through the tree, a vortex of whirring. One dips down for a snack, a split second of calm, a sip of sweet through a needle-thin bill.

The regular feeder is empty though I filled it two days ago. "Can't they keep a secret?" my mother asks of the voracious sparrows.

Hints of spring burst at the end of thick, dark branches.

Finches dive in and out of the jasmine that's climbing up my window.

I gave Luna a marrow bone from the freezer so she wouldn't be bored while I was at work. Where Before she could spend hours outside gnawing away, her bone remains untouched until I return and then she wants me to stay out with her. Or at least leave the door open while she chews.

She will try and bring it in the house. I tell her she needs to leave it outside, and she puts it down and I open the door wide and then she quickly leans down to grab it and make a dash. We can go back and forth like this several times before she deposits the bone just outside the door and comes in. If she does this at night, she will get up two or three times to check on it.

Luna doesn't like closed doors. When my younger son is home and listening to music or the TV and I close the door because background noise feels like rats scurrying in my brain, she will get off her mat in my room, push open the door to the hallway that leads toward his room, and rather than turning around and coming back to her mat, she will circle the whole house and open the other door I've closed that leads to the kitchen. Once the doors are open, she will settle on her mat again.

Chapter Seven

It is seven thirty in the morning. The doors and windows are open, and the warmth is starting to creep in, clinging onto the tired desert moisture smell from the few drops of rain we had last night. Mostly, I wake up and find my bed much the way it was when I slept. Often, making the bed involves nothing more than stepping out of it and flipping back the covers. Today, however, my bed is a mess and reminds me of when I would wake up at TWMIL's house, in his bed, in his arms, when it felt like forever in both the magical and the difficult ways. He would hold me, and I'd feel safe and loved but also wonder where the me who had first walked into his house had gone. He didn't have enough furniture for me to hide behind, so I was probably outside somewhere with the weeds and the lizards and the birds. I'd go out in the early morning to look and I'd catch glimpses of the me I knew.

"Hey girl," I'd say.

For a moment or two we would reunite, but mostly I'd keep going in this state of loved and hidden and when I would run into her—me—it would be like when you bump into someone from high school who remembers you better than you remember them and you are sort of happy to see them but you don't have the energy to reconnect.

Sometimes the universe steps in. Sometimes it doesn't.

My older son was hit by a truck and in a split second everything exploded into bits and scattered for miles.

I am still picking up the fleshy pieces.

❧

A month after the accident I called the DPS sergeant who was in charge of the investigation and told him I wanted to see where it had happened. We agreed to meet at the McDonald's a few miles east of the spot and drive in his vehicle to mile marker 229.2. I was shaky on the twenty-minute drive. TWMIL and Noreen both offered to come with me, but I needed to go by myself.

Just before the exit, a hawk flew in front of the car at window level. Was it the same hawk that had flown in front of us at window level as we passed mile marker 229.2 the day after the accident on our way back from breaking the news to my younger son?

This day, the sky was a sharp blue and laced with those poofy clouds that reshape themselves into dragons and birds and ships.

Sergeant Blue was waiting for me in the parking lot. He was white, average height, thick around the middle, and had a small mustache and a high and tight. He carried a black computer case and could easily have been playing a cop in a movie. We went inside and sat at a booth and chatted while he pulled up the report. He planned to retire in two years and wanted to live on a beach, making him the fourth white man in law enforcement or the military I have encountered who has voiced this exact retirement plan. He went over the report with me and then pushed the computer my way so I could read it for myself.

He got up and ordered a combo meal.

I read.

He came back and ate, and I talked about Raad, often tearily. I showed him pictures. He said he was a handsome young man, that he *looked better without the goatee and mustache*, that he was very sorry for my loss, and that it must be devastating.

After I had finished reading and he had finished his burger and fries, we went out to his SUV. He reattached the computer to the console area and turned on the ignition. Tejano music blasted from the radio.

"That was unexpected," I said, even then grateful for the reminder that you never know about people.

There was something light about the afternoon, like maybe we were going to go off in his SUV to the secret world where a very alive Raad was spending his days. This was a legitimate possibility in my mind.

I resisted the urge to rock, which I have done off and on since I was a baby when stressed and/or forced to sit still. My mother was worried that I had autism when I was young. As an adult I learned that rocking is a mechanism to cope with stress.

Driving at exactly the speed limit—"if they catch us speeding, it comes out of our paycheck"—I looked into the side mirror and saw a cargo plane but when I turned to look for it out the window, I could not find it in the sky. A trick of angles. Also, a sign—Raad had loved planes since he was a very young boy and could identify just about anything, like this C-130.

I told Sergeant Blue about the signs, about the owl that had flown over me a few days Before.

"We had a Native American guy who worked in our office," Sergeant Blue said. "There was a huge tree out front where an owl would sometimes be perched. This guy wouldn't leave the building if it was there."

I didn't tell him about the swan that had come out of the water near my younger son's rehab a few days After and how a young man had tried to hit it and kick it and how I had screamed at him like a madwoman to stop.

We continued driving and several birds flew over and around us in winged escort. We pulled to the left on the highway and then made a U-turn through the median and up to the spot where they had found what was left of my older son. Sergeant Blue stopped the vehicle and gave me a reflective vest . . . I get stuck here because I cannot remember if he gave me the reflective vest in the McDonald's parking lot or when we got out of his truck on the highway. Cars and trucks whizzed by us at seventy-five miles an hour and I could see how easy it would be to step out and think you could make it across those three easy lanes, totally misjudging speed. Three lanes of highway are not much wider than the quiet street I live on.

Sergeant Blue pointed out the dozens of white paint spots on the road that marked where they found pieces of Raad's head, "none bigger than a quarter." Sergeant Blue kept walking and stopped further up and said, "this was where his body was found," lying at an angle facing northwest. ("It's just the body," Kevin, the funeral director, told me before I went into the room with Rula and Noreen to say my goodbyes to what was left of my firstborn son. *It's just the body.* I would replay these words thousands of times in the following months and years.) We walked along the median, he on the outside of me, while vehicles sailed by us. Debris loaded the edges of the road, car parts of all sorts, raggedy things that once were whole, a shocking amount of unidentifiable items in plastic and metal, most colors dulled by exposure to the elements into a variant of gray. (When they gave me the manila envelope containing the items they found near his body, there was a studded leather bracelet that I am certain was not his.)

It had been a month since his death. I was calm as I walked with Sergeant Blue next to me, looking at the debris along the highway where Raad had taken his last breath. I nudged a piece of tire with my foot and turned it over. A full month and several rains after his brutal accident, the tiny silver olive tree charm that had been hanging around his neck when he had taken his last step lay perfectly intact by the side of the highway. I leaned down and picked it up. Even though I had not yet started the medicine, my heart was calm.

"What is that?" Sergeant Blue asked and seemed confused when I held my hand open and explained, with cars and trucks passing us at seventy-five miles an hour, that this tiny delicate thing was *the charm you had on your necklace.* How could it have remained a month in this violent spot by the highway, undisturbed? The necklace that held this charm had been returned to me in the envelope. It was broken and blood-stained.

I held the tiny tree in my hand, again resisting the urge to rock as we drove back to the McDonald's. Sergeant Blue offered to help with anything he could, said that I could call him anytime day or night. I wondered how many times he had made that offer and how many people had taken him up on it.

We got to the McDonald's and I thanked him. We said goodbye and I drove away, not quite ready for the freeway that would take me home. Instead, I crossed into a nearby neighborhood. I looped up and down the quiet streets while a handful of clouds formed themselves into Johnny Cash. I took a picture in case I started to think I had imagined it.

As planned, I drove to Noreen's house. We had both moved to Tucson at the same time, when our older sons were four, in order to raise our kids closer to our mothers. For weeks after the accident, Noreen came to my house every day. She organized a meal train. She talked with the Loft theater, the place Raad found joy, and arranged to have the memorial there. She kept me from . . . from what? Losing my mind? Falling into the abyss? Noreen told me that there was nothing she could do to change things or make it better, but she could soften things for me in places.

That day I drove to her house and sat with her and her husband, John, who had coached Raad's soccer team for years. I told them about the visit. I opened my hand and showed them the charm. She gasped.

These things happened. We all saw them.

Chapter Eight

"Let's go to the Middle Eastern Studies party," Houri said one fall afternoon in 1990.

She pushed and cajoled until we made our way to the tenth floor of Bunche Hall, a short walk that would alter the course of my life. The small space was filled with people eating catered grape leaves and hummus and felafel and drinking and chatting. A colleague of ours was there with his newly-arrived-from-New-York roommate, someone he had known at Birzeit University.

The roommate was tall and balding and had a thick mustache; he was older than me by almost a decade. While he would become very dark and serious over the years, when I met him, he was easygoing and smiley, smart and funny and kind. We talked for the duration of the party and the next months unrolled with him settling into Los Angeles and us settling into each other. He job hunted and I finished my master's degree. I moved in with him and we explored Southern California. We walked and talked and made plans.

On a Friday morning two years after we met, the man who would become the father of my children, my husband for seventeen years, to love and to cherish, to have and to hold, in sickness and in health, for richer or poorer, *till death do us part*, called in sick to the factory job he had finally found, and we drove downtown and got married by a Black woman judge who wore bedazzled white sneakers.

We went out for Chinese food afterwards.

We spent the next years weaving a life together with threads that reached around the world and tied us to one another. We lived in small spaces and enjoyed each other's company. We grew into each other. We never had much money and on Friday nights we would sometimes get the two-for-one pizzas from the tiny joint around the corner from our apartment. Raad's birth opened something up in my husband, but it also closed off something else, something that would never fully reopen, even with the birth of our second son almost four years later.

We were living in a one-bedroom apartment and doing our best at parenthood. We worked and took hikes and went to parks and the beach and to Third Street Promenade where we spent hours in Barnes & Noble. Raad attended a sweet community nursery school connected to the university. We took him to car shows and airshows. We cooked and celebrated and laughed and played.

Our West Los Angeles apartment felt like it was getting smaller and we explored possibilities. Pasadena? Austin? Ramallah? Tucson?

Things were good until they weren't. The slow boil of our falling apart may have begun before our move to Arizona, but it was there that the literal and metaphoric heat went up, a slow more-than-simmer that finally boiled over against the bookshelf my mother built in the dining room.

"Why would anyone get divorced?" I had asked aloud early on in our seventeen-year marriage.

He would never kill himself.

I would never know a boy with lace-up shoes lying dead in the rain.

Why hadn't the universe listened?

Or had it?

Chapter Nine

"You are a force of nature," TWMIL told me as things were heading toward over. He said this in the way my father called me *'aasifa,* storm, the way men call women *unreasonable* and *crazy* when we state our needs or get frustrated.

TWMIL loved me. It was not his fault that after losing my first-born son I did not want to hang out with people I didn't really know or go to bars and avoid many topics that mattered to me, that I no longer wanted to drive for endless miles so I could frolic on a beach, or wander in a wash, or explore a mine, or tile a floor. I had done those things with him and enjoyed them because I enjoyed him, but now I wanted to be silent and alone in familiar territory or with my family and close friends. I wanted safety, familiarity, and purpose.

How does me standing up for what I need make me a force of nature?

Nature is wild and man tries to control it.

"Well, according to the Bible, the Old Testament," Rhody says, "if you name it, you have power over it. Dominion."

Nature is pure and man adulterates.

"Why do people need to get in with wild animals?" Carolyn had asked me when I told her that TWMIL wanted to take me to Mexico so we could swim with sea lions. "Why can't we just respect their space?"

"You are my greatest accomplishment," TWMIL told me.

All my life I was led to believe I was too much.

Too talky.

Too loud.

"EEEEH!" my ex-mother-in-law exclaimed and slapped me, a mix of playful and hard, when we were walking in the village and I cracked up laughing. "Men can hear you."

Too emotional.

My mother told me that I did not have the right to my father. She did not distinguish that while she did not have the right to him as a man, I did indeed have a right to him as my father. That blurring of the lines that began before my birth carried on into everything.

I do not blame her, though I did for years and years.

Because I come from two worlds, I am very good at taking on whatever the person I love takes on. It was a survival strategy and began with my mother. The knowledge that I was in error, *ghalta*, was woven into me before birth and would surface if I were to disagree, to be different, to want something unexpected. This is why I am so good at adapting to other people. My core self—the one who shows up in love and motherhood and writing—she stays true, but all the surface stuff is very flexible.

Until it's not.

I am in my fifties and shame wends its way through my story like a contaminated river.

"When we are safe and comfortable, we lead with our heart," says Khalid. "When we feel threatened, we become our details."

"You are the greener grass," TWMIL told me a few months into our knowing.

These were words I could trust.

"White-man-love is a leash keep me from soaring; maybe it's just man-love and got nothing to do with white," I wrote a year and a half into knowing him.

In reshaping my details so people can see me in a way they can understand and not get caught on surface stuff, I am not trying to please; I am trying to survive.

I lie to tell the truth.

Chapter Ten

Some months after Raad died, between his graduating high school and turning eighteen, my younger son started using drugs again.

One night his bedroom window stood ajar, waiting for his agile figure to hop back through.

I closed things up. Anyone's agile figure could come through that window.

Rock, paper, worry.

He went on a tattoo bender and got five tattoos in the space of ten days from a friend of a friend working out of his house.

I chased drug dealers away from our house with a stick, as though they were wild dogs and not stupid boys with guns.

"You need to leave the state," Rhody said more than once. "Get him out."

Not long after that, we stuffed ourselves into the tiny white car TWMIL and I had flown to Las Vegas to buy from an optometrist after I had T-boned the black Corvette, and headed toward my aunt's house in Maine, in what would turn out to be more than 6,000 miles of a slow, round-trip escape.

We exhaled the dry desert air and inhaled Santa Fe cool. We found our footing in Jambo Restaurant and Gift Shop while we waited for a table, enjoying the wooden figurines and jewelry and household items and spices and foods and music. I asked the man who ran the store for the name of the song that was playing—"Niambie" by Harmonize—reopening my scabbed-over love for Afropop. As the man and I chatted about music, I felt like myself for the first time in months. Years. When our table was ready, my younger son and I went into the restaurant and he devoured two and a half plates of stew in what felt like home and hope and healing.

We exhaled ashes and worry and inhaled Colorado Rocky

Mountain highs. We stopped in Trinidad for lunch. The town was a hilly cluster of red brick buildings that stretched into rural as we drove further north. We stayed overnight at a motel on Freedom Road and I purchased weed from a dispensary, carrying Marwan's philosophy that this could save my younger son's life if it kept him from the harder stuff.

We exhaled Trinidad weed and inhaled Hays steak and potatoes served by a young waiter who would go on to remember us when we returned two months later. We exhaled amazement at the number of adult stores along the highway in Missouri, and inhaled Lake Erie from atop a picnic table. I exhaled falling leaves alone on a quiet pathway in upstate New York while my younger son visited his father. Together we inhaled the Piscataqua Bridge and exhaled Cranberry Island.

We settled into my aunt's house on Clark Point Road and helped her dislodge forty years of living. I got to know her as a person without the complicated family dynamics of mothers and daughters and sisters. My younger son slept and ate and slept and ate. I rested and wrote and went for walks and ran and explored and talked to myself and to Raad. With Noreen on the phone, I sprinkled some of his ashes into the crisp water of Norwood Cove.

"You have joined the awful sisterhood," my aunt told me. She too was a member, though my cousin had been a grandfather when he died.

My younger son had been applying for jobs online and was hired as a ski lift operator in Colorado, starting in early November. We left my aunt's house and stayed outside of Portland where we ordered marijuana to be delivered to the parking lot of a hotel. We visited friends and family in New York and New Jersey and Pennsylvania. We revisited moments of my childhood. We drove by the Bryn Mawr house my mother grew up in and the house on thirty-two acres of land that my aunt had lived in with her second husband. We wandered the boardwalk in Ocean City and bought each other rings.

We had lunch with Becky, a friend from college, and her husband Bob. "We have a house in Richmond that is just sitting empty. Why don't you stay there until you need to leave for Colorado?"

The next day we drove to a suburb of Richmond and began our month's stay in a quiet house that had two living rooms.

My younger son slept and ate. He got his wisdom teeth pulled without medication.

We drove all over the state.

We went to a private zoo for depressed animals.

We passed emergency rooms with wait times posted on their neon marquees.

We visited every Goodwill in the area.

We went to museums and wandered through woods.

My grief followed me around like an unruly puppy. Sometimes I'd hold him in my arms and he'd comfort me. He'd bark at anyone who got too close, peeing and shitting wherever he wanted, chewing up my favorite shoes.

My grief slept with me, snuggled in close, kept me warm, wouldn't let anyone else share the bed.

An empty bed is a beautiful thing if you want to stretch out with your thoughts and memories.

An empty bed is a difficult place to step out of.

We stayed in Richmond for a month in a luxurious and optional version of the isolating we would later experience during the pandemic.

Linda, the teacher who had helped get my younger son through high school, had drawn him a picture of a tree with birds flying out of its stark branches. It was a symbol of Palestine, of Raad, of our family, and of life. Before he started his new life in Colorado, my younger son wanted the tree and the birds tattooed on his forearm. He went to three different shops to interview artists. He chose Jess at Heroes & Ghosts, partly because she talked about the picture excitedly and from an artistic standpoint instead of just as a business transaction.

I dropped him off on a Saturday afternoon and left to wander. I walked away from the commercial area and when I turned the corner at Ellwood, a raggedy Lhasa apso ran up to me.

We chatted a bit and I picked her up. She was cuddly and affectionate. There were no people around. I sat down at a table and chairs in someone's front yard and read her tags, dialed the number while Angel sat on my lap and no one answered.

We sat like this for a while, Angel and I, greeting passing pedestrians and talking like old friends. A man came out of the house and I asked him if he knew whose dog she was.

"I am watching her for a friend."

He took Angel out of my arms and retreated into the house.

I walked back to the tattoo shop. My son's forearm looked brilliant.

My younger son and I ate together and saw movies and talked and enjoyed each other's company. We crisscrossed the country and carried Raad with us. We drove through snow and rain and brilliant sunshine. We remembered Raad stories, cried over him, held him close. And we repaired a lot of what had been broken between us.

I stayed in a Vail apartment we rented and wrote and started to learn alone while he settled in the way a kid going to college would.

Early one morning I said goodbye to him after breakfast at McDonald's and headed home alone in my little car that TWMIL and I had flown to Las Vegas to buy. I stopped at a hotel with a heated pool in Blanding. I bought a rotisserie chicken at the grocery store across the street and whitish-pink nail polish at the Dollar General next door. I went back to the hotel and put on my bathing suit and swam alone in the heated indoor pool. And then I ate dinner and painted my nails.

Some kind of cloud action is happening in this Utah sky. Six nail lines scratched out some holes in the dim white, found the magical orange hiding out in the background. Birds fly in formation the shape of wonderful.

You are here.

You are in the glorious huge of the Utah sky, in the sulky hawk on the power line, even the crows eating off the highway.

You are everywhere and in the quiet I know this to be true.

Chapter Eleven

Bloody threads of blame spatter across the highway of this story. Each one must be photographed and documented, cleansed and prayed over before it can be disposed of properly, by incineration.

I blame everyone and everything; we are one after all.

I blame the night, the earth, the seas.

I blame Donald Trump for getting elected and voters for choosing him.

I blame Barack Obama for having given Raad hope.

I blame the sun for rising and the sky for seeing and doing nothing.

I blame life for not being easier.

I blame the truck driver who didn't see Raad until he was already there.

I blame the world for not being more hospitable.

I blame the talking that overflows the levees and drowns me.

I blame choking on stories.

I blame the stories themselves.

I blame Israel.

I blame their father for leaving them.

I blame unfulfilled promises.

I blame my knees for hurting.

I blame my father.

I blame hope for coming into our lives in the form of white partners.

I blame our foolish red hearts for taking the bait.

I blame the bait.

I blame not measuring up and not knowing our worth.

I blame the roads that lead in and out of now and promise something else.

I blame the tired engine that doesn't think it can.

I blame the nighttime that is my namesake but couldn't save my older son, even as I am grateful to her for releasing her death grip on my younger son.

I blame everyone for their ignorance, my father for selfishness, my mother for never letting go.

I blame Raad's friends for not reaching out at just the right moment.

I blame myself for letting my guard down.

I blame myself for impatience, for being annoyed by such small things as being woken up or having to wash an extra dish.

I blame myself for only seeing the hawks but missing the owls, and I blame the owls for getting the message wrong.

I blame myself for being impressed by the ferocity of wild animals while not fully recognizing their destructive power.

I blame myself for trying to choose ease.

I blame the sitcoms that got it right in a way that made sense to all of us: *Everybody Hates Chris*, *The Fresh Prince of Bel-Air*, *Reba*, and *Kim's Convenience*.

I blame Leslie Knope for not intervening.

I blame writing for her siren call.

I blame fear for wearing a disguise and settling into me.

I blame my poor detective skills for not seeing her true colors.

I blame expectations for soaking through the fortifications of our sweet home.

I blame all of us.

I blame no one.

❧

Carmon asking her mechanic to pray for me and her messages that she is holding me close provide comfort.

"Raad was clearly someone who knew love" feels like an embrace.

I find solace knowing that Brent had had strong thoughts of Raad come to him the morning Before and that Carolyn feels honored to share his birthday and is "grateful to have gotten some of his film insights."

"Things happen for a reason" hollows me out.

"You were the one person who did completely right by him" holds my head above water.

Rula's "I miss hearing you talk about him" is home and Marwan's musing that "perhaps God was protecting him from something worse" sands down the edges.

I am comforted by the thought that Raad was a brilliant, loving, kind human who touched the lives of many people and the knowledge that I was a good guardian/caretaker for his spirit/soul.

Now he's on the next phase of his journey.

There are daily reminders of this: the birds, the light and joyous quirks of the universe. Even the most rational of his friends agree that *Moonlight* winning the Oscar a week After was Raad's behind-the-scenes doing.

I am comforted by the feeling that he is free.

There was or there wasn't, a long time ago, a bird prince in the shape of a man.

Chapter Twelve

Luna and I visit the park every morning so I can talk to birds and ghosts and she can run around and roll in the grass. We began this ritual in the months After when, leaden with missing Raad, I struggled to drag myself out of bed. It was a different park then and we'd return to TWMIL's house.

"This is Bowzer, with a 'z.' He's great with all dogs," the slim, pale man in sunglasses calls out as a heavyset pit bull trots toward Luna.

"She's hit or miss," I respond, though really, she's 95 percent miss.

Bowzer and Luna circle each other with a few feet between them.

"Bowzer reads other dogs and mimics their behavior so they're more comfortable. You should see him in doggie daycare. He's really good at bringing the shyer types out of their shells."

"My dog isn't too social," I say.

"My dog will try to bring her out of her shell," the man says.

Bowzer sniffs Luna who has her tail tucked deep between her legs. He circles closer. Luna is rooted firmly to her spot, lips curled up, teeth bared, a low rumble coming out of her whole self.

"Bowzer, come, that's enough."

Bowzer ignores his owner.

The man looks across the park. "I have been wondering what that guy has been doing," he says.

I follow his gaze and see a man walking while a dog trots at a distance in front of him.

"I just realized he's had his dog off leash this whole time and it's been running in and out of the oleander." The man shakes his head with an edge of disgust but since his own dog is running off leash, I don't understand.

The man he's talking about is slim with dark skin and dark hair; his head is slightly down. There are no oleanders on this side of the park, and while there used to be some at the base of the hill, they've been gone for years. I am stuck on this inaccuracy and the edge to the man's voice.

"Bowzer, come!" the man says again.

Bowzer ignores him.

"Everyone has their personalities," he says with a chuckle, as though he's figured out a secret. "He's just learning her."

The other night I watched the first few minutes of a documentary about Ted Bundy, which I turned off because who needs that sort of stuff in their head? It was a good reminder that you never know about people.

Bowzer circles us with self-confidence. If he were a man, he'd be one of those cheerful guys who goes to the gym and pumps himself up to gigantic. Bowzer's owner is still talking about dogs and personalities, about Bowzer being so good at reading people. Luna is further away now, her tail returned to its normal position. A couple more minutes and she and Bowzer might play, but the man intervenes the way neurotic parents do, "Oh no, Bowzer, come here, leave her alone."

"They're fine," I say. "They're off leash and she just needs a minute."

"They all have their personalities, don't they?" the man says, smug and stiff. Neither of us have removed our sunglasses to have this conversation. "Bowzer, come!" the man calls with a sharpness to his voice.

I say something to Luna about it being fine and everyone's just playing. "Have a good day," I say and turn away.

Bowzer walks by my side. He wants an in with Luna.

"Bowzer, come!" the man shouts, and my dislike of him overwhelms me.

"Come on, Bowzer," I whisper. "Come with us."

The man's voice rises shrill, "Bowzer, come!"

He's used to being obeyed. I wonder if he is like this with girlfriends or boyfriends or children.

"Come on, Bowzer," I whisper. "You know you want to play with us instead. Good boy." I keep walking. Bowzer is undecided, following along but at a slower pace. "Good boy, Bowzer," I say.

Bowzer makes one more playful lunge at Luna when the man full-on screams, "Bowzer, now! Or you won't get your treats."

Bowzer stands and watches Luna cross the park. The other man who *had his dog off leash this whole time* is looping in front of us; his head is still down as though he's lost in thought, perhaps also remembering a son. His dog comes to greet Luna. They sniff each other and both continue on their way, as does the man, as do I.

Salt and vinegar almonds make me think of you.

Remember when I asked you to buy me some—"enough to fill the container I keep them in"—and you thought I meant the giant ceramic cookie jar and you bought three pounds of salt and vinegar almonds? Even the cashier asked you if you really wanted that many. You'd think we'd still have some.

Our electric kettle plugged in makes me think of you.

Remember how you always said it had to stay plugged in even if it was off because it kept the water warmer? I would tease you by unplugging it and you would plug it back in.

The red toaster makes me think of you.

Falling asleep in front of a movie makes me think of you.

Chris in Gentefied *makes me think of you.*

Christian Cooper makes me think of you.

Al Pacino always makes me think of you. That moment we saw him with Houri in Santa Monica when you were a baby was when you caught the movie bug.

Looking at your posters makes me think of you.

Walking by the back door makes me think of you.

I am still waiting for you to walk in.

Chapter Thirteen

The other day I was in Target and a woman with waist-length gray hair was standing in front of the cheeses. She apologized for taking her time and I told her not to worry and that I will say "excuse me" if I need to get through because life is too short to be waiting on someone else's cheese decisions and she laughed full and smiled and said "take care" and I said "you too" in that way of women knowing each other and embracing with words that really mean *I got you, sister* and *I've been there* and *stay strong.*

"Everything is about the connections," my aunt told me over dinner during the weeks my younger son and I stayed with her. She had prosecco, I drank red wine, and my younger son smoked weed. Dinners were very peaceful.

When I lived in Los Angeles and took the city bus, I would come home with stories of the people I had seen, the things they had done and said, and always, the nuances of their conversations and actions. The ones that carried quiet weight became poems. The louder ones, the kinds of stories you'd expect to find on a Los Angeles bus, did not. I talked about all of them with a physical need to discharge the information. My husband said that I was the only person he had ever met who could ride the bus for twenty minutes and talk about it for a half an hour.

A decade later, during the falling-apart years of my marriage, those sorts of interactions—that took place in grocery stores rather than on the bus—kept my head above water, reminded me that there were other forces in the world and that I was not alone.

"It's great that people feel they can talk to you about anything," Raad had said many years ago from the back seat of the car I would eventually total. One of the Trader Joe's cashiers had followed us out to the parking lot and was talking about the mother of his daughter throwing him out again and the subsequent bender he had gone on. "You can't have your cake, throw it in the dumpster, leave it there for days, and then expect to eat it when you want to," he had said, still a little drunk.

"It's great that people talk to you about everything. Except when we are trying to leave," Raad had said. "Then it's terrible."

❦

One morning when I went swimming before things fell apart, Nick was bustling around with prickled energy.

"How are you?" I asked.

He stopped, his reading glasses at their usual crooked angle. "You know, sometimes life is really hard. It's just hard."

I agreed.

I thought I knew what he meant.

He went off to deal with his demons and I slid in the pool to drown mine.

Chapter Fourteen

When we came to Tucson, my mother had considered moving into a house on the eastside, but while she was taking a tour, a man had come over and introduced himself and said he was a shoe salesman.

"How was I going to survive in a neighborhood surrounded by shoe salesmen?" mused my brilliant mother who never wore makeup and whose currency was her mind.

My mother was like Google and could answer accurately any question I ever asked her. About anything. Kazakhstan. Spider behavior. Philosophy. History. Anyone's history. Weft and weave of rugs. Astronomy. Gravity. Tax law. Math. Any western painter. Minutiae about the Middle East. Anatomy. Politics. She is Shipley, Radcliffe, University of Pennsylvania law school brilliant. Greek mythology, the Bible, philosophy, history, and my grandfather's colorful tales of his difficult upbringing—he was born poor at the turn-of-the-previous-century to Scottish immigrants in Kensington—are the basis for her understanding of people.

"Do you know the story of Narcissus?" my mother would ask me when I was young and she caught me looking in the mirror. She would go on to remind me that Narcissus was so enamored with himself and his own beauty that he spurned everyone around him because he was busy gazing at his reflection in a pool of water, next to which he eventually turned to stone or withered away.

My takeaway was supposed to be humbling, that I shouldn't be absorbed by my own appearance. What it ended up doing was make me believe that something awful would happen if I were seen clearly, either by myself or anyone else.

When you are different, when you cannot find yourself in your surroundings, you want to understand why. And if you cannot do that, you may never know how you are seen.

You thought you were white.

The small, midtown neighborhood we eventually moved into was mostly white (including immigrants from France, Switzerland, and Germany) and filled with intact families; of the sixteen houses on our street, eight of them were occupied by professors or people in some way affiliated with the university. There were enough children on our street to play a very long round of Ghost in the Graveyard.

I became immediate best friends with a girl in my neighborhood whose Mexican musician father played soccer with her and her brothers and spoke to them only in Spanish. Their Uruguayan mum was a math teacher and terrific cook and there was always a surplus of tasty food in their house.

Unlike my silent home with books and uncomfortable furniture, people were always coming and going, in Spanish and in English. Many times I'd be over there when they were about to leave for some event or another, and while I was rarely invited to go along, her mother often asked me to wrap whatever present was laid out on the long cherry dining table. I credit them with my ability to speak Spanish and to wrap presents.

I spent every day at their house until the dreaded five o'clock phone call when my mother would announce "it's time for Laila to come home" and ring off without interacting with whoever had answered, triggering jokes and mimicking from her and her brothers. For decades.

Here we are riding our banana seat bikes through giant puddles after the rains.

Here I am sitting quietly in her cool darkened living room with the white carpet while she practices piano.

Here we are as teenagers walking in on one of her brothers getting a blow job in that darkened living room.

Occasionally, I would stay for dinner or spend the night. In the early evenings, her mother would read on the couch while her father played piano. We called each other *sister* and yet so much about her life was different from mine.

On Christmas morning we were always best friends. We would

check in on each other early early to compare gifts—I always got books and she always got musical instruments. Later, after I had breakfast and her family had their Madera from tiny gilded glasses, we would go around to the houses of the other kids in our neighborhood to marvel at their Christmas fantasyland of fur coats, guinea pigs, and Pachinko games.

Here I am driving my best friend to school and to soccer practice.

Here she is with her clothes ironed smooth and her shoes cleaned of scuff marks.

Here she is spending forty-five minutes to curl her hair.

That's her getting drunk for the first time with me and then being forbidden to see me.

And that's me getting drunk at her quinciñera.

Here I am as a bridesmaid at her wedding, along with her grade-school best friend Mikaela. That tall thin blond girl she met in college is her maid of honor.

Our friendship flowed in waves and just like that barn dance, I never let go, not when she made fun of me about being goofy looking and having to go home at five to take a bath and read a book, and about having a very different sort of mother, not when she had better things to do, and not when she ignored me.

I never let go.

Over the years we grew into ourselves and outgrew the details, and in so doing, we settled into being proper best friends, talking regularly and seeing each other a few times a year, including our annual pilgrimage to stay with her and her husband as she moved from one suburb to another. She would stay with us whenever she came to town. The boys knew her as one of their aunties.

She upgraded cars and downgraded husbands, splitting from her gentle high school sweetheart to marry his opposite, a Marine-turned-contractor who, in one of the first conversations I ever had with him, said that there was no real difference between cops and criminals except for the law and that contractors lived the best of both worlds. When we drove with him in Phoenix one afternoon, he pointed at a Black man crossing the street and said he was a criminal, pointed at an Asian man and imitated him.

He drove by what he said was a gay bar and talked about AIDS. He renamed my kids Jim and Paul because it was easier. And he routinely mocked Mexicans.

In spite of this, my growing-up best friend and her husband seemed to be living a happy life, traveling and entertaining.

And then her story went dark.

Her husband accused her of having an affair. Her parents and I begged her to come home, worried for her safety. She stayed. Her husband forbade her to contact any of us, in what felt to me like him yanking her out of the snaking rows of dancers, pulling her home through the darkened woods by her hair and locking her in his stinky lair.

Did everyone have barn dance issues?

At this writing it has been almost five years since I've seen her or talked to her.

❧

My walls have always been porous. My drawbridge has always had broken hinges. I used to be okay with visitors; I enjoyed the company until the Cedric Diggory moment, the it-can't-be of most impossibles.

Months after Raad became dead, the days had groaned back to routine: my younger son snuck cigarettes when I took a shower, TWMIL wanted my attention, my mother was unbearably sad, and I felt squeezed by everyone.

I retreated to the open halls of my grief where Raad hung out and none of that outside noise tugged me away. I distracted myself in my work with refugees, and their so many more bags of trauma. Sitting on my bed, rocking slightly, I read about PTSD. "She demonstrates rhythmic movement of her arm throughout the interview," the text told me.

Death and trauma are sledgehammers to the smooth plate of clear thinking and imagination. All those glorious pieces scatter themselves across the yard, giving the same momentary effect as finding a perfect seashell on a crowded beach. They mostly turn out to be incomplete lovelies, flashes of beauty, and sometimes deadly shards that slice through even the roughest of heels. They will never come back together as they once were. The best you can hope for is a mosaic mash-up held in place by some pretty grout.

I do not have a victim card in my deck, though sometimes I double-check. Sometimes I fake it for a few hands.

The assumption I was white allowed me privileges I am still unpacking.

Some mornings I wake up white. On those days I order dresses off eBay.

Some mornings I wake up Occupied. Those are the days I walk uncovered with the sun—which no self-respecting brown person ever does by choice—and I listen to stories and rescue cacti and landscaping materials and furniture from the alleys behind my white neighbors' houses.

Felix, the electrician who installed a couple of ceiling fans and whose son was joining the Army, said he'd never been treated badly for being Mexican—except for the one time early on in his being here twenty years ago when an older white lady threw a hamburger at him in McDonald's—but he also thought people shouldn't spend too much time caught up thinking about that stuff.

The weekend after we had that conversation, a white man shot up a Walmart in El Paso, specifically targeting Mexicans and other people of color.

TWMIL also said that people shouldn't get so caught up on their superficials. He greeted non-white people in what he presumed to be *their language*, no matter how many times I cringed, told him it was offensive, and explained how patronizing and superior it came across.

"How is me showing I am open to them offensive?"

From the beginning, I accepted him, military, guns, NRA membership, and all. I stayed and I loved him and I accepted his love and it was true. And yet, with Raad dead, those things were at the root of me needing to distance myself from him.

The first fight we had, more than a year into our knowing, was about Sandra Bland. He said she shouldn't have talked back to the cop.

I will light you up.

And I lost my mind.

Some years ago, I met a white writer. His writing was lovely and solid but then I read an article he wrote where he referenced his non-white partner from whom he was estranged. His portrayal was graphic and intimate in a National Geographic observer sort of way that felt like betrayal. I was incensed.

Often, the fault we find in others is that thing we most loathe in ourselves.

A hummingbird wears his shimmery green robe as he hunches forward over his breakfast. Once he leaves, the bees descend, cluster at the joining between clear glass and red plastic; their buzzing is too much for my head.

First sparrow of the day, feet clenching the dark, dry mesquite bark as he extends his short self toward the yellow tray. The alert has been sent out and in an instant the tree is filled with the jittery motion of sparrows.

In the dry of our desert, even green looks parched. Bark pulling away from itself, thin branches full of crack and dust.

I feel like this sometimes. Skin pulling away from itself, thin bones full of crack and dust.

Does my body carry the aftermath of death?

The next-door neighbor's bamboo used to be lush. There were times when all eighteen of our tombstone roses would be in bloom. Herds of finches hanging out, their tiny yellowish bodies smooth, their movements sweet compared to their coarse cousins. Sometimes Raad would run outside and throw a rock at the bamboo to shut the chattery sparrows up.

Everyone texts and I want nothing to do with any of them, but then they get busy and I drown in lonely.

Everything feels like an assault.

I am broken inside.

The male cardinal is here. Another bird chases him off. Why? There is enough for everyone.

Chapter Fifteen

When I was living in Jordan, I'd visit Amman on the weekends to see my father. One night he took me to Pizza Hut for dinner, most likely an effort to avoid all places where he might run into someone he knew and be compelled to refer to my fictional *himaar* of a father. We were sitting in his Mercedes and he had been drinking. "I loved your mother," he told me. "She is one of three women I loved in my life. I told her she should have had an abortion."

Ghalta.

Even though I was the "x" in this algebraic equation, a system of calculation created by my 50.7 percent ancestors, I was not considered on the fuller side of those parallel hyphens.

Or I was considered but only as a delicate figure that needed protecting.

Or as an extra letter that was fucking with the equation.

Was I a refugee?

An immigrant?

An American?

I wanted clear answers that no one could give me.

When I was in graduate school, I decided to seek help.

I made an appointment with a counselor at Student Health, and on the day of the appointment put on my Kevlar: loveliness in the form of a long, drop-waist, patterned dress. As I sat before what I can only remember now as an old white man and broke down the details of my story, saying I just needed an answer I could give that was not a lie but that also answered the dreaded where-are-you-from question, this man looked me up and down and said "I notice you are wearing the covering style of dress of the Middle East. I wonder if you are ashamed of your body."

§

I was given American citizenship at birth because my mother was a US citizen. I should also have been giving Jordanian citizenship at birth because my father was a Jordanian citizen.

Like my grandfather, my father was also a man of status, but with him I was the daughter of a family friend no one had ever met. Maybe I was a girlfriend. I was not his daughter in anyone's eyes, and I could claim nothing, could ride on no one's coattails.

My father's family name is particular to them. If I Google the name _____ I can be fairly certain that I am related to whatever face pops up.

And there are a lot of faces, in Jordan, Palestine, and in the US. I do not exist for any of them.

Among them are Olympic athletes, artists, writers, models, fashion designers, attorneys, physicians, and nominated royalty.

I recently came across a picture of my father and King Hussein in their late teens or early twenties. They look as though they are playing dress-up in their fathers' suits. My father is six inches taller than anyone else in the picture and his face is Raad's face.

My father's family has a golf course and a school on their property. They host outdoor concerts in the summer months.

The internet has only amplified my awareness of the family's wealth and status.

Ghalta.

I hope one day you will be proud to say I am your father.

There was or there wasn't.

Whatever real estate and financial security I have is thanks to my mother and my grandfather. And TWMIL.

Raad was overwhelmed by the Arab relatives, though he enjoyed visiting Jordan where he could live a quieter, more polished mahogany time.

Arabs were his closest friends.

Raad loved suspenders and country music.

Raad looked just like my father.

If he had lived past twenty-one, he would have had the time and space to explore these different worlds that were his.

You were working your way toward brave. Had you lived you would have been even more astounding. You started to launch but then you returned. I used to say that this town was a place people come to die in. Was our house both a joyful home and something to escape?

When I was leaving Jordan, the American lady I sometimes stayed with—the one my father said "is not a woman" because she rebuffed his usually drunken advances, and who may or may not be a librarian living in Fairfax, Virginia—gave me a silver keychain with an Arabic coffee pot on it. I took the coffee pot off the keychain loop and hung it on a long silver chain that my mother had brought me from a trip she took to Yemen. In my late thirties and beyond, that necklace became daily wear, replacing my gold necklace of charms that held the baby ring my father gave me, the map of Palestine, and the pendants my in-laws had given me when I got married.

On our last day after a month in Richmond, my younger son and I went with Becky and Bob to a diner that made delicious fried chicken sandwiches. Later, in Crozet, when I got in the car after saying goodbye to Pam, I realized my coffee pot charm was missing. I panicked. I called the diner. It must have gotten caught and fallen off—I did vaguely remember catching my necklace on a corner of the red metal table—the woman said she would look and call me if she found it.

We drove and drove and at the next stop I got out. Wedged between the seat cushion was the silver coffee pot.

It had fallen between my legs.

✦

Shame taught me to rock only when no one was around, except when I am the passenger in a car for a long ride, then I let loose. I got chicken pox one year when I came home for Christmas. My husband told my mother he knew I was sick because I didn't rock at all on the entire seven-hour drive back to Los Angeles.

Recently, when I sit with my younger son at dinner I rock back and forth in my seat. Sometimes he asks if he's done something to upset me.

I am sitting in my bed with the dog near my feet reading this on my laptop and swaying gently forward and back, forward and back. In the limbo before graduate school, I lived in St. Louis and exchanged an attic apartment for childcare. Something had happened in my day and I was very upset, raging upset. It was freezing outside and nighttime and I had nowhere to go and I couldn't scream or bang on walls, so I rocked. I rocked vigorously on my hands and knees, something I hadn't done since I was a child, since I had learned to modify my rocking by sitting up and moving my torso to and fro in silence. The woman who owned the house came up and knocked on my door, said there was a terrible noise in the ceiling and was I causing it? I denied it. I denied it denied it denied it.

I was mortified.

I still am.

Chapter Sixteen

Even though I have three jobs and am a single mother of 50.7 percent color, I have privilege that includes enough time and space to do yoga in the morning and walk the dog before work.

It's predicted to be eighty today even though it snowed a couple of days ago. The dog seems tired, is panting more than usual, and coughs in a way that concerns me.

We get to the park and enter from a bit further north than usual. I wonder if our vermillion flycatcher friend will find us. *There he is!* a fantastic punctuation mark sitting at the end of a barren white branch that hangs low and alone on a tree. *Nature's emoji.*

There is a man in a hoodie with a sleek black dog that runs toward us as we cross the field. Luna looks nervous. The man calls out that the dog is friendly; Luna bares her teeth. The dog comes right up to her and she growls and snaps. The guy is young, *your age.* He giggles and we agree to let them work it out.

"This is Dex," he says. "He's one and a half."

For the next five minutes we watch Dex and Luna sniff snap retreat approach repeat sniff snap retreat approach repeat and finally play.

So many potentially positive encounters have been thwarted by nervous owners who don't give their dogs time to work things through, who run away at the first snap.

"I've had more problems at this park," Dex's owner says. "People actually cursing me." Dex has a device on his collar that his owner says is a shock collar "but doesn't shock. I tried it on myself just to make sure. This is helping me train him. He used to run away and not come back."

After several circles around the field, Dex's owner marvels that Luna is so spry at ten. "She is great," he says. "And loves you so much."

That her love shows makes my heart swell.

Luna hurls herself into the prickly grass and scratches her back.

I have not seen her do this in the presence of another dog in years.

The first time I tried to do a free-standing headstand, I fell heavy on my wood floor.

I began practicing against a door. For just in case.

And then I got it.

With my head and forearms holding me up, I could make sense of the world. When I switched back to right-side-up I felt so very good.

Until my neck stopped turning.

"Yeah," the nurse practitioner said. "With that arthritis, you'd probably do best to avoid headstands."

Another morning waking up to find you gone.
Another morning waking up with birds twittering and chirping,
feeling you are close.
Another morning waking to the realization that all I know is gone.
Another morning forcing myself out of bed, wondering why an-
other morning. Wishing for a rewind button.
Another morning replaying your last day on earth.
Another morning imagining your last moments.
Another morning with stones filling my belly.

I took the dog for a run that turned into a fast walk because of my knees.

On the way home, I found an old, corded telephone and picked it up to use as a prop with some future class. As I went up the stairs to my house, I looked toward the university. At the tip-top of the giant pine tree halfway down the block in the yard of the Latino man with Trump yard signs, there was what looked like a stump rising up. I stared and it moved and the dog and I walked toward it and I saw the distinctive long neck, beak, feathers of a heron, a great blue heron.

Your favorite.

A heron in a desert city is impossible. Okay, there's Sweetwater some miles northwest and the zoo a couple of miles to the southeast so it's not impossible impossible, but it is super unlikely.

I walked down the street, giddy with amazement, tears brimming. I watched it adjust itself, take a periodic peek down at us. I stopped a couple and pointed it out. "We are from Maine," the woman said. "We see herons all the time and that is definitely out of place." The man took a picture on his phone. I thought to ask him to send it but felt foolish and didn't.

I used to take pictures, so many pictures, so I could relive events five minutes after they happened. My ex-husband took over the documentation of our lives. I have boxes and boxes of photos, all documenting a life that was mine but no longer seems real.

Chapter Seventeen

I had coffee with Careema on her porch.

For more than a year After, she texted me every single day and kept her cell phone on and next to her bed. *Call anytime.*

Careema's house is lovely. Every fixture is thought over, every touch intentional. When I was married, I compared myself/my household to her/hers and always felt like I fell short; now I enjoy her creativity and artistic eye. Her across-the-street neighbor came over to chat. He used to have a shed on the far side of his property and when he sold the lot, he took the shed apart brick-by-brick and rebuilt it brick-by-brick closer to his house.

He beamed as Careema told this story.

"I used to have the biggest crush on you," he said, smiling. "I'm not gonna lie. You'd walk by my house reading and a lot of times you wore them tall boots and I had the biggest crush."

I never had tall boots.

I do, however, have a pair of work boots that are so heavy they make my legs tired.

During the time around my divorce, I was drawn to heavy boots, the kind you would wear if you worked with large animals on a muddy ranch. I had no extra money, two young sons who were with me most of the time, and a myriad of expenses; work boots could not be justified. I thought about them for months, looked in stores and online. Tried on a few pairs. I probably talked about them. One day my frugal mother handed me an envelope of cash that would have bought her two weeks of groceries and I used the money to buy a single pair of Frye boots, my version of a superhero's cape. I thought—with each heavy step I took on the half-mile walk to and from work—that these boots would carry me through the difficult times. I thought I could kick away any evil that got near me.

And I have a witness.

No way to know that the difficult times had yet to come and that no accessory would be powerful enough to carry me through.

Chapter Eighteen

The violence that reverberated through our lives was like stones in a hurricane and I was a tattered flag connected by threads and flapping uselessly.

I had nightmares when I managed to sleep and visualized ways I could die when I was awake. In the first weeks and months After, I thought it was because I missed Raad so much. In later weeks and months, I thought it was because of the alcohol. Then I noticed that the missing was less self-destructive if TWMIL was not around, as though his presence uncorked some primal and awful blaming connected to Raad's death, even as he did so much to help me manage everything, even as he was loving and mostly patient.

I couldn't make sense of what felt like my body declaring itself by roping in my nervous system.

"I think I am depressed," I told TWMIL in the months After.

"Of course you are depressed," he said. "You need to get out and do things and you will feel better."

Get out and do things!

Depression is a shed in the corner of the back yard.

When depression is dormant, it sits in its corner loaded with cobwebs and old crap you think you might need one day. It's been there so long you don't really see it anymore.

When depression awakens, the shed has somehow moved closer to the house. It is cleaned up, more appealing. You can't help yourself from wandering out there to poke your head in for a quick check. Maybe you carry a glass of wine to the shed for a few minutes of quiet. It has a couple of windows and your people look out from the house and see you in there and wonder what you could possibly be doing. You pop in from time to time so they will know you are fine and then before you know it you are out in the shed again, only now it's just a spit away from your back door. You'll just be there for a few minutes, you tell yourself. You just need a minute to sit or maybe have a lie-down on the floor.

Everything goes gray in your tiny clapboard shed with aluminum windows that doesn't offer much beyond shelter in a rainstorm. You might glance up toward your house, but the effort required to make your way back in is more than you can muster. Sometimes the door of the shed vanishes. The windows get smaller and you can't quite see out and you decide to have another lie-down on the floor but there is a thunderous banging on the walls and you pull yourself up to sitting and see your younger son smiling and suddenly you are in your room and he is sitting at the end of your bed pointing out a hummingbird and he keeps talking to where he convinces you to get up and go with him on a drive and for the rest of the evening you manage to stay out of the shed.

§

I woke up missing TWMIL. Even as the awareness of missing crept in and the "what if" wandered across, I dismissed it all.

Live for the living.

You are stuck. You need a push.

Why when I am lying in the shed does my mind go to him?

Dopamine.

Dopamine deficit disorder sounds more medical and controllable than *depression*.

I believed that TWMIL would protect us.

I believed my mother would protect me.

I believed my husband would be around for the long haul.

Expectations not based on reality.

I believed Raad would live a long and full life.

And this should have been.

I believed my younger son's struggles would smooth out with love.

My expectation of life did not involve so much suffering.

And where the fuck did you come up with that idea? Certainly not based on history.

Based on the myth of America.

Based on the myth of successful, white America.

How does that relate to you? You are America's bastard child.

I look for statistics to help me make sense of this, but I cannot find myself anywhere.

In the United States, less than 10 percent of children were born illegitimate in 1966. Less than 2 percent of white women ages 30–34 had illegitimate births. I do not have statistics for Lebanon.

In all of these studies, illegitimate children fare worse in health, academic performance, and behavioral issues.

But I did not think I was illegitimate and I was not treated as though I was illegitimate.

Does that make me less illegitimate? More legitimate?

While my mother was not married, her father supported her.

My mother had a law degree.

My father had a high school diploma.

On my way back from dumping the recyclables, I glance at Luna's water bowl. A pale white moth floats on the quiet surface, a delicate triangle.

I dip my finger in the cold water, scoop it up, hold still for a few seconds then place its waterlogged and immobile self on the bench to dry.

Luna and I stand side by side watching.

I nudge the moth with my finger. Nothing.

"I think we are too late, Luna," I say.

My seventy-pound dog who has charged at other dogs from half a block away and bitten holes in her sister's flesh sticks her giant black nose at the back of the tiny moth and snorts. The moth jumps and then, looking like a drunk nun, ambles across the bench.

Luna looks up at me and turns to go into the house.

Chapter Nineteen

I knew another Raad. Raed was a tall Iraqi boxer and student with deep acne scars. He was rough around the edges but there was a purity about him, a rawness that made sense to me. He was direct and shameless, which also made me trust him.

I was seventeen, taking classes at university, and hanging out with my older Arab friends.

We went dancing one night at Voilà, the nightclub where all the Arabs hung out.

I had a spectacular fake ID, spoke with an accent and a movie star attitude, a combination that got me past bouncers for years.

That night, shortly before my high school graduation, I wore the elegant white linen dress my mother had bought me for the ceremony with strict instructions not to wear it beforehand.

Toward the end of the night there was commotion by the entrance. A young man from the Gulf had returned to the club, showed the stamp on his hand as proof he had been there before. The bouncers refused him. A scuffle ensued.

Somehow this information drifted inside the club to all of the Arabs who then became indignant and righteous.

My memory is a jumble of movement after that. Raed punched the bouncer landing a few drops of his blood on my dress.

Years later I ran into him. I remember little of that evening, straddling him briefly when everyone had left, kissing him, saying we weren't kids anymore, that we couldn't mess around just to mess around.

He agreed and we separated.

I never saw him again.

Raad wanted to see Bruce Springsteen when he came to Glendale in 2012. The concert was on a Thursday and no one he knew was going. Since he had only just started driving, there was no way I'd let him drive to the Phoenix area on his own.

After many angsty conversations, I agreed to take him.

We packed ourselves into the blue SUV in the middle of a weekday afternoon and headed west. My younger son and I dropped him off at the arena and went to the nearby mall to watch a movie, though I can't remember what we saw. It was December and there was a massive Christmas tree set up. After the movie we drank hot chocolate in comfy armchairs and stared up at the tree, and then we went to the car and slept while we waited for Raad to get out.

Sometime after eleven, Raad strode across the parking lot exalted, giddy with energy, and for a good part of the drive home he talked about the concert and also about the fans and what a genuine community they were.

When we feel safe, we lead with our heart.

When Raad turned eighteen, I gave him everything on his wish list.

I enjoyed shopping for and ordering each thing, reveling in the extravagance of it: all the Criterion DVDs, an Xbox, clothes. He also asked for a belt buckle. I looked online and in stores but found nothing that suited him. I happened upon an artisan's fair by the train tracks. One tent had handcrafted, silver belt buckles. The Navajo man who was there with his wife and two children told me that the one I was holding was a perfect choice as the bear signifies strength and family.

Raad wore that belt buckle every day—except on the days he was wearing suspenders or sweatpants. He died wearing that belt buckle.

Our family wasn't strong enough to protect him.

On the night of Raad's first birthday After, I had two nightmares.

In the first I dreamed of my ex-husband's rage. He was like a wild animal as he tore through our house, tackling me. I screamed for help from TWMIL who was standing nearby. It was the gurgled suffocated scream of the sleeping. I broke through and woke up before anyone could do anything.

In the second dream my ex-husband and I were in our house and the couch was missing. He said he had destroyed it. Detectives came to the door. He spoke to them, wouldn't let them in, was vague in their purpose.

Raad was dead in both of these dreams.

Your cold, dead hand was the last part of you I touched.

It's just the body.

I sit next to the dog and gently rub the crusted globs away from her eyes, which Raad also did and I wonder as my fingers rest on our dog's face—the dog who chose him—I wonder if my creaky fingers hold his spirit.

You always said our dog could see ghosts.

Part Two

Ships at a distance have every man's wish on board. For some they come in with the tide. For others they sail forever on the horizon, never out of sight, never landing until the Watcher turns his eyes away in resignation, his dreams mocked to death by Time. That is the life of men.

Now, women forget all those things they don't want to remember and remember everything they don't want to forget. The dream is the truth. Then they act and do things accordingly.

—Zora Neale Hurston, *Their Eyes Were Watching God*

Chapter Twenty

The year Raad graduated high school he wanted to buy a car. While we all helped him with advice and forwarded advertisements—TWMIL in particular—Raad knew what he wanted and when he found Gloria (a red 2003 Nissan Frontier) it was love at first sight. He hung an air freshener from the rearview mirror with a picture of a pinup girl on it (later the subject of one of my younger son's five bender tattoos) and kept a billy club under the seat. For just in case.

When I was finally ready to sell Gloria three years After, Thabet considered buying it, but ultimately decided on an F-150.

My younger son bought his boss's Nissan Titan when his boss upgraded to a Dodge Ram.

According to one study, more than 80 percent of new pickup truck owners are male.

There is a man down the street, young, my height, who has a truck that is so tall you might need a step to reach the runner where you can stand to get in.

TWMIL traded in his nearly new truck and bought a double-cab *for the fam* and then after we split upgraded to an F-150 four-by-four because the previous truck wasn't large enough to accommodate his needs.

TWMIL had an old, hard double mattress when I met him. He agreed that softer would be better and purchased a queen mattress that he put on the floor with the plan of building a frame for it. When I was away for those two months, friends gave him a king-sized metal bed frame and he purchased a king-sized mattress to go with it because he remembered how much I had loved the king-sized bed in the hotel we stayed at in Atlanta the night he almost died from an asthma attack.

That bed was like its own country.

The first time I went to Mexico with TWMIL we were walking on a beach—he is massively gifted at finding beautiful, deserted locations—and we wandered in the warm sea and held hands.

"I can't wait to take you to the Bahamas," he said.

"We are here in Mexico, naked on a beach, let's just be here," I said.

I don't remember what he said, but he was irritated.

My ex-husband was not extravagant but when he bought things, he also went big.

There was the orange extension cord that reached from here to Palestine that my younger son accidentally cut through the other day with the hedger.

He bought brackets for a shelf he was making that would have been—in the words of the builder who added our porch—"good if he were constructing a house." After he moved out, I found nails that could hold a man to a cross.

He planted four blue Agave Americana, two in the front and two by the back gate. They can grow to have a six-to-ten-foot spread with three-foot spiny leaves. I had the front two removed when he moved out. The two in the back are mammoth and I routinely have to trim back their "sharp teeth and terminal spines" with a saw. We have all been stabbed by them as they are too big for the space they are in.

When we bought our house, the backyard was bare. We planted eighteen tombstone roses, three Chilean mesquites, and an acacia tree, not realizing that half of the roses, two of the mesquites, and the acacia had thorns. In the difficult years, I was not paying attention to the irrigation and many of the rosebushes died; only seven remain. I have scars up and down my arms from years of pruning because while my husband planted them and watered them, he never pruned them. The mesquites have three inch "variably dangerous stipular" spines that Raad would trim off with small clippers when he was young and collect in a tiny purple plastic bucket that once contained colorful chalk. The purple bucket sits in the dining room on top of the other bookshelf my mother built.

The day their father was leaving the state and came to say goodbye, Raad walked through the house with a sledgehammer intended for his father's car. I stood in front of him and gently coaxed it away from him so he could stand with his father on equal footing, but there is no equal footing between father and son. I did not protect Raad in that moment from anything other than making a spectacle. When he told this story on the night before he died, he said that he wielded his sledgehammer.

"You don't understand testosterone," my younger son said to me recently. "And I don't think you are remembering the story right."

Maybe mothers can't understand the ferocity of sons, the bursting of emotions that breaks furniture like bird bones.

Perhaps it is because we are the ones cleaning up the debris.

Chapter Twenty-one

The first of my post-divorce series of unfortunate choices was a career-military bald white man who was rugged and handsome. On our third or fourth date, I met him for lunch at a restaurant I had frequented as a teenager. I walked in through the gift shop where, as a kid, I had spent many dollars and countless hours poring over interesting knick-knacks, greeting cards, and off-the-wall books.

I stepped into the front part of the restaurant where I saw my date sitting. I stared at him. He looked different somehow, carried an unfamiliar energy. I froze, confused, and pretended I didn't see him while I collected myself and looked through the window toward the outdoor seating area behind him where my actual date was sitting by himself at a table for two. He waved at me. I looked back at the first man. He smiled.

I went and joined my date.

This man wrote long, clever emails, philosophized about life, and was generally quite pleased with himself. He had never been married and had no children. He was sufficiently unavailable that I suspected he was dating several women. In the course of our short dating life, I had five or six nightmares, one in which he appeared as a demon. I was not yet listening to my Knowing so I noted them and kept going.

My lemonade arrived and I blew my straw wrapper at him. He pulled back and his face tensed like he was about to scold me.

A few months into our sporadic dating, I attended the funeral of Rula's friend, Margie, a social activist and a counselor, someone who had devoted her life to healing, love, and nonviolence. Reading through her obituary now, I think I would have liked her very much if I had known her today. I had too much going on then and still carried around my suitcases loaded with *you don't measure up*. In her calm presence I was aware of my too-muchness.

I sat at the back of the church with Thabet while Margie's close friends and family celebrated her life, the gift she had been to so many communities of people. Someone read excerpts from a letter she had written to her granddaughter. It was long and involved and encouraged her to know her own power and worth. "Stick with men who love you truly and be wary of men who just need you. And if you don't get it right the first time, get it right eventually."

I bawled.

When we left the church, there were slips of paper hanging from a tree for us to take.

"In order to do more, I must stop more; and that an increased voice requires an increased silence."

I considered retying it and taking another one: even in death Margie was judging me.

I went home to get ready for my date with the man I could see clearly now was a terrible choice for me. I danced around my sweet house listening to Tupac and adding kohl to my reddened eyes. My date picked me up and squinted at my music choice the same way he had squinted at my straw wrapper assault. I said goodbye to the dogs and off we went in his fifty-thousand-dollar SUV to share a hundred-dollar meal at a South American restaurant I hadn't known existed.

The restaurant was lovely, fancy and comfortable at the same time, and not the kind of place I had been to in many, many years. I felt strangely relaxed as I sat on a bench across from my date with Margie on my right and Tupac on my left. My date asked me what kind of wine I liked and when I answered "red" he looked at me with that same squint, the one that not only noted difference, but disapproved and tallied it.

When I told Raad this story later, he shook his head smiling. "Oh, Ma, you are so ghetto."

I felt light, carefree.

My date spent many minutes with the pretty young server

folded behind him, their faces inches apart, going over the wine list like it mattered and using words I would look up when I got home: tannin, Malbec, Syrah.

They looked cute together, but I suspected a server at a restaurant was beneath his standards.

Tupac was giggling. Margie was holding my hand.

I sat calm and confident, girded by two ghosts as I looked into the handsome face of a man who had no real interest in who I was; I was not at the point where I could admit to myself that I had no real interest in him for more than what he represented. When the waitress came to take our order, he requested an extra plate of "plantations" and I pinched myself to keep from laughing out loud.

Tupac stood up like he was going to leave. "Girl, the fuck are you doing with this fool?" He stood for a few seconds staring at me. "You know what?" he said and sat back down next to me. "You enjoy your fancy plantation meal."

I don't remember much else of dinner, other than the food being really good, especially the plantains, and Margie and Tupac giggling and showing varied degrees of indignation at whatever topic my date weighed in on.

I did not offer to pay for my meal or even to cover the tip, which is not how I am, not with friends, not with dates, not with family, and not until many, many months in with TWMIL and only because he found my offering annoying.

People turned as we walked out of the restaurant past a bank of mirrors; we both looked confident, attractive, and completely not right for each other, in what I thought of then as a diplomat and her bodyguard sort of way.

We got into his SUV with the heated leather seats and headed down through the city, Margie and Tupac whispering together in the backseat.

When we pulled up in front of my house, I turned to him and said, "You don't make me feel amazing."

His blue eyes stared at me in the dimmed light of his fancy vehicle. "I don't make you feel amazing?" he leaned his head into his hand in a sort of Thinker-in-a-car pose. Even his reaction felt not real.

"No," I told him. "I had fun tonight and have enjoyed hanging out with you, and thank you, but no, you do not make me feel amazing."

I stepped out onto my street. Margie and Tupac were standing on the sidewalk near the corner.

I looked at the moon and walked back into my life, feeling a little sad, but also relieved, and free.

Another exercise I like to do, both with writing classes and with groups that I am training or working with, is create a scene in the middle of whatever I am doing or talking about.

I might, for example, be talking about the importance of active listening when a colleague will walk in wearing a scarf, a glove, and carrying a couple of items. The person will turn around on the stage to make an announcement, do a jumping jack, drop something, and then walk away.

I will ask the assembled group to write down exactly what happened and to include all the details—colors, sounds, movements. When they are done, I will read a script of the person's actions and ask people to circle the information that they had and draw lines for anything they left out.

Then we debrief.

In the many years I have done this eyewitness exercise, with the hundreds of people I have done it with, only one person has ever claimed to have had all the facts. She was in a group of one hundred plus people so I didn't challenge her, but I never quite believed her.

Chapter Twenty-two

I am stopped at a red light on Sixth and Sixth. A man is halfway across the crosswalk when the light turns yellow and he breaks into a trot. He doesn't look anything like Raad but is close in age and dresses like he's trying to figure it all out in blue chinos and a button-down shirt and he's holding a water bottle that's meant to look like it's made out of wood. I've seen those at stores and always laugh that anyone would spend thirty dollars for any kind of water bottle but then I could see Raad doing that very thing and then the man hops up the curb in front of my car and I look at his hand holding his looks-like-wood metal water bottle and in that split second the road opens up and swallows me.

"You are so sensitive," my boys would tell me.

They hate this about me because sensitivity trickled down to them. It shows up differently in each of them, but they've both got it. Raad came off tough, like he'd got an edge, but one impassioned conversation and he'd be teary. The younger one plays tough too, in a different way, but he can see people's intentions clear as day, so he hurts a lot. My boys had their bones shaken up when their father and I split, recurring earthquakes in their souls, the pits of their bellies carrying daily aftershocks.

The first time I went swimming many months After and saw Nick, he bounced tense on tiptoes, like he knew what was coming.

"I haven't seen you in a while."

The story poured out. Part of it in Spanish because it was safer. Nick cried the way Mohyeddin had cried the way Jon had cried the way Santiago had cried.

Sometimes a man's tears are gifts.

Sometimes they are lies. A creepy cop I dated had shed crocodile tears in my living room.

And sometimes they don't make sense, suggestions of behind-the-scenes happenings to which I have no access. TWMIL teared up in my backyard before he said he loved me for the first time.

TWMIL had written a novel. He showed me two or three notebooks that contained his lifetime of writing. When we emptied out my garage, I piled up the two large plastic bins filled with my notebooks and writing-related materials; this did not include the two shelves of notebooks and research materials in my house.

"This is my writing stuff," I told him.

He stared, clearly surprised. "Oh wow, you are serious."

As though the three published books, four not-yet-published books, and discipline to write every single day was not enough proof.

What gives you the right to edit my words?

There is a groove worn in the dining room table where I've laid my head; that is how long I have been at this.

Do you tell a river to stop flowing because it's in your way?

Become the river.

When my younger son was in grade school and struggling, I found a therapist for him who would have me come in alone and we would strategize approaches.

One day I asked him if I should stop writing—my kids were eight and twelve then—and maybe focus on more tangible life things. Maybe try to earn more money.

"When you are at the bus stop and that is where you sleep, then maybe you need to revisit. For now, you are teaching your children bravery. You are doing this thing that you believe in and know you are good at and you are honoring that. Most children learn bravery from their fathers."

Do they?

The cop I dated briefly who wore swim trunks instead of shorts was at my house one afternoon and said something off-the-wall to me, something I knew not to be true in a gaslighting sort of way.

I didn't want to argue with this man in my house when my children were there, so I went into the kitchen. I stood at the sink and breathed and looked at the knives in the dish rack and thought about stabbing a knife into my hand.

This was a sensation and thought I had never before experienced. I literally stood at the kitchen sink and thought about picking up a knife and stabbing it through my hand.

"Why swim trunks, Ma? In case a pool comes along?" Raad had asked.

"Do you know why white men wear swim trunks?" my younger son asked me recently. "Because they don't have to wear underwear."

Another writing exercise I like to do with students is have them write from the perspective of an object that someone has.

A knife in the dish rack, for example.

Or swim trunks.

❧

A few months before I met TWMIL, while the boys were visiting their father during winter break, I had coffee with a heavily tattooed man who worked as a nurse in a prison. He was pleasant. Attractive. Well-read.

On New Year's Eve, a day after our hot chocolate date at Starbucks, I was giving our three dogs end-of-the-year biscuits. Bella, the four-pound chihuahua with only three working legs, jumped into Luna's space. Luna growled and nipped at her. Luna is seventy pounds. Her nip caught Bella at the neck, jerked her very hard, and threw her up in the air. Bella landed with force onto the tile floor, quivering at an impossible angle. She was a few breaths away from dead. I could barely look at her. I wrapped her in blankets and put her in the garage and apologized. On New Year's morning I dug a grave for her by the west wall.

Do Not Stop For Hitchhikers

I never saw the tattooed prison nurse again.

In winter, my skin is gingerroot in color. In summer, I turn nutmeg, or cappuccino. I run in shorts and the sun paints thigh-hugging tights on my legs that I can wear all year round.

Once when Raad was a baby, we were standing at the counter in the Arabic grocery store and the owner looked back and forth between us. "Where did the darkness come from?" he finally asked.

From his father.

From my father.

My older son carried my father's face.

His grandfather's face.

My older son carried a story he could never tell.

My older son is dead and will never tell another story.

To master a handstand, you must first prepare your wrists and shoulders.

Over time you will build up mobility and core strength.

Practice frequently, daily if possible.

Have a goal and a plan. Sure, you want to master a handstand, but what does that mean? Do you want to be able to hold a handstand for a certain amount of time? Do you want to be able to walk on your hands? Are you trying to improve your form? Straighten your back?

Be specific.

Train regularly but for short periods of time. You don't want to overstrain your wrists or elbows or shoulders because then you will have to stop practicing until they heal.

Build up for endurance.

Always practice mindfully, paying attention to your movements as you are in them, even if they are repetitive and you have done them a thousand times before, but also, don't overthink it.

If you still aren't mastering it, get a coach.

Chapter Twenty-three

I was on my way to swim and stopped at the Shell station. A young man at the next island asked if I could spare a dollar or two for gas and I told him "sure, hang on a sec," and I got my pump going and went over to him and asked him if he wanted me to fill up the tank and he looked surprised and said "yeah, that would be great" and I ran my credit card and told him "go for it" and he smiled and I could feel his sweetness and I walked the eight feet back to my car where the gigantic sadness overtook me and I turned my back to him so he wouldn't see that I was crying. Something about him—his sweetness perhaps—reminded me of Raad and I finished filling up my tank and throwing out the trash that had accumulated over the week just like I would have done any other day and I got in my car and he said "thank you again" and I drove to the gym so I could swim and maybe find some comfort in water and movement but really everything felt insurmountable.

Later, I went to the mall to pick up my prescription sunglasses.

There were only a few cars in the lot and as I opened the door a young man came up and asked for gas money. He had an elaborate story about not getting paid on time and not being from here and wanting to drive home. One of the things that most irks me is when men approach women in faraway corners of parking lots and ask them for money. For a split second I considered giving him money anyway and then got irritated all over again at his bullshit story and I told him "sorry, I don't have extra money now," which was true because I was unemployed. The boy and I walked next to each other for a little bit which reminded me how nice it is to do errands with company and he said again how hard things were and before I could respond and tell him *son, don't go up to women in the parking lot like that*, he had woven away through the cars to another woman who had just pulled up.

I went inside to pick up my glasses.

The lady at the store was polite in the way you have to be if you have a customer service job, but behind her nice were knives that she had sharpened on my first visit when I went with TWMIL and my Groupon that promised us each a pair of single-vision prescription glasses for forty dollars, which is cheap unless you have no income. TWMIL had been talking for months about needing a new pair of glasses and I was excited to give him a functional and needed gift.

"I've never seen this. We cannot honor it," the woman had told me when I handed her my phone with the coupons.

"I paid for them; I can't return them, and it says it's good for this store." I was polite, but I know my rights as a customer. Also, this is not some little mom-and-pop glasses store; this is a national chain.

"I've never seen it. We can't do it."

"I have already paid for it," I told her. "It guarantees I can use it here and we need glasses."

She mumbled and then discovered a stronger voice and said that she would have to "follow up with Corporate," an expression I didn't think existed outside of *The Office.*

While I went in for my eye check-up, instead of browsing for glasses, TWMIL talked her off the panicked ledge my coupon demands had sent her out on. "I won't get any glasses," he later told me that he had said to her. "That way it will just be the one coupon and you won't get in trouble."

When I came out from my exam, I sensed some version of this had happened by his total lack of interest in the glasses on the wall and their awkward eye glances at each other. Because I have not totally outgrown adolescence, I asked him in front of her what glasses he had chosen. He said he'd tell me later. I nodded in that way I do when I don't believe you. Any of you.

Because I have trust issues.

I picked up my glasses, walked back out alone into the sunny parking lot with my eighty-dollar-desperate-boy sunglasses, and headed home.

§

On my birthday, just over a year After, the dog and I went for a run. While she pooped, I stared at the sky. It was a glorious morning with clouds and drizzle. A cluster of birds held themselves in the sky above us and then spread out on their way. Ravens, perhaps. I counted them. Twenty-seven. Then thirty-eight. More. Forty-something. Could there have been fifty-one? One for each of my years? Raad's birthday offering!

Later that day, TWMIL invited me for a walk in a rural area an hour's drive from us that I have always loved. We wandered and talked and things were a bit strained but we have always been good at wandering and enjoying one another in silence and open space. We stuck to the dirt road while the dog ran off in the fields chasing rabbits and ferreting around. We heard her yelp. When she finally managed to limp back in our direction, her ankle was swollen and she couldn't put any pressure on it. Luna and I sat on the dirt road while TWMIL went back to get his truck and pick us up. Instead of turning around and going back the way we came like we usually did, we continued driving up the road we had been walking on.

TWMIL was driving slowly and leaning out his window and driving and looking. "What is that?" he asked after several minutes of this.

I sat up in my seat and craned my neck but couldn't see anything.

He stopped the truck. "I think it's an owl," he said.

"No way," I said.

We both got out. Leaning up against the side of the road was an owl—freshly dead and twisted. What are the chances that an owl just falls dead out of the sky by the side of the road where there are no trees and we happen to come across it?

He leaned over and pulled out a feather and then kicked it further off to the side where it wouldn't be hit by any oncoming vehicles. This did not seem a respectful ending for it but—like so many other times—I couldn't find the power to say anything.

"It's telling you to let go," TWMIL said and handed me the feather.

Of you, I thought.

We got back in the truck and I was quiet as I turned the feather around in my hand.

"Sometimes we get attached to being sad," he said.

He said other things, but I cannot remember what they were because I was so stuck on the impossibility of this scenario. Not impossible like when Raad was killed when he was supposed to live a fulfilling and long life. This was impossible like I wondered if TWMIL put the owl there, set the whole thing up, had planned for us to keep walking and happen upon it.

But why would he do that?

Did he think I was so influenced by bird things that if I saw an owl and he told me to let go that I would just magically get over the death of my firstborn son?

And where would he have gotten the owl?

And why would anyone go to such an effort to create this scenario?

And had Luna sensed this and tried to thwart it by going off and getting injured?

It all seemed unlikely.

And, as he would come to say repeatedly, I have trust issues.

We went home and walked into his house where Noreen and Rula and Thabet and Victoria and Rhody and my mother and my younger son were all inside hiding in wait with food and bags of bird food—the gift that TWMIL instructed they bring so I could get lost in watching all the birds frolic in my yard. Luna limped around to each of them and said hello. I fell into the love of these people, my family, and even though TWMIL had arranged it all, I felt impossibly far from him and could barely look at him. And even as I could barely look at him, I felt awful for it.

One afternoon I met TWMIL for lunch after going for a walk and then a swim in an effort to calm my soul. So many hours are involved in calming my soul. While swimming, I fantasized about the roast beef salad I was going to order, and the coffee I was going to make in the quiet of my house once I got home.

When I got to the restaurant, TWMIL had already ordered me a sandwich he knew I liked as well as a coffee.

I ate the sandwich and didn't finish the coffee. I ordered a roast beef salad to go.

I didn't apologize for either of these things.

How can I enjoy being treated like a queen and then resent it because it undermines my autonomy?

❧

From one of my notebooks:

We are around the corner from the first anniversary of Raad's death. My insides are like popcorn in the wind in a sandstorm in molasses.

My white boyfriend is paragliding in Colombia.

I have regained wisps of stability: employment, exercise, a schedule.

My younger son is coming home. I want to be excited, but he has been flying through money and the last time he was home he stole things and I chased drug dealers away from our house with a stick.

I wake up alone after five hours of sleep with a clear memory of the last four years, of the impossibility of it all.

My white boyfriend is paragliding in Colombia.

My belly is swelling up the way it does when the stress is too much, when my intestines take on what the rest of me can't handle.

My white boyfriend is paragliding in Colombia.

My younger son who has been working steadily in another city for the last three months preceded by two months with family and friends away from here, quit his job yesterday before I had a chance to go visit. I want to believe—oh, how I want to believe—that he is simply homesick, that I am not going to find him with a sledgehammer at the safe where I have learned to keep my computer and my car keys.

My white boyfriend is paragliding in Colombia.

Chapter Twenty-four

Squirmy birds fill my tree with their sweet movement. Reds and browns and greens and yellows and twitters and chirps fill the air. *You would enjoy this. I can hear your voice, "Ma, come look. No, Ma, come look again, it's different now."* Is reveling in that joy "indulging sadness and dwelling in the past"?

I think not.

A woman came into the clinic yesterday and talked about her house chicken.

I thought of you immediately.

Amazing how one comment rewinds me to a back stoop with my two beautiful boys and a lovely life.

Our footprints pave a path to the park, the library, the video store. Walks to and from school. To and from work. Walks with and without the dog. No breadcrumbs required: our footsteps are weighted with history.

Our village has spit us out one by one.

Even though my mother was a lawyer, I did not read the fine print, the promise that promised no promises. The one that said America dreaming is just that. My privilege was not active currency.

To be denied your story is a second cousin to being denied your country, an auntie to being lied to about who you are. Trauma of origin.

Yesterday I spoke with a woman in her late sixties who has been doing the same job for forty years. "I can't believe my life is almost gone," she said, her painted-on eyebrows in two clown-like peaks.

I have been struggling with my eyebrows. They've always been light and they thinned out after my bout with West Nile virus. Or maybe it had nothing to do with the virus and they have been falling away with age.

"You don't want to make your eyebrows dark," my mother who never wore any makeup informed me in the way she had said not to lie or steal or cheat or shave my forearms or pierce my nose or sing to my children or keep pictures of old boyfriends. She told her own truths as though they were absolutes. And I couldn't see the difference.

I like my face better in darker eyebrows, but I've noticed that sometimes if I'm not paying close attention things can get out of hand.

"Those are pretty severe," my younger son has said more than once.

There is an eight-by-ten black-and-white picture tucked in a corner of my room. In it, my hair and eyebrows and eyes are thick and dark, exaggerated by makeup and product. I am wearing a cotton dress with a couple of buttons undone at the top of the form-fitting bodice. I am facing the camera with one leg resting on a stool and a hand on my hip. I look strong and fierce and lovely. The picture was taken by the sister of the friend who ended up sleeping with the man I thought of as my first serious boyfriend, who pushed my head between his legs when I came to reclaim another picture she had taken of me.

I was interviewed by a woman of mixed/divided/blended origin. "I read some of your poems and for a while, you thought you were white." She laughed.

I might as well have thought my father was a king.

Expectations are traps.

Some we set ourselves.

The author of "a seminal Arab American novel" shalt not play in America's sandboxes. At least not with American boys.

The pendulum of expectation won't leave me alone. Even with one son dead and another mending.

"Now you can write," people tell me.

Is your life ever your own? What does it mean for something to be your own? Your child. Your family. Your story.

It is no wonder checkpoints make my heart beat faster. *Is everyone in the car a citizen?*

I was told I was too emotional and that was wrong, so I stored the emotional up and it turned into the always-providing soup-pot living inside my belly.

Can we teach our body not to sweat?

Normal respiration is twelve to sixteen breaths per minute. I can get myself down to three. My heart offers less than sixty beats per minute.

And so what?

My stomach twists are the result of decades of high fat doses of untruths my system cannot digest or expel, leaving me puffed up and floating.

Untruths I took on and repeated.

When I was young, I wanted my father.

I wanted siblings.

I wanted to stay with my grandparents. Sometimes I wanted to live with them.

I wanted to be closer to my cousins.

I wanted a room with privacy. I wanted space.

You cannot have these things, I was told repeatedly.

I wanted to learn Italian.

I wanted to live in Italy.

I wanted to be Italian. *Nell'intimo, sono italiana.*

You may have to reinvent yourself.

I wanted to cut hair for a living. To dance for a living. To write for a living.

I wanted five children.

"What do you want?" TWMIL asked me early on in our knowing.

"I don't know," I'd answered.

"How can you not know what you want?"

How could I be a fully formed human and not be in touch with my wants? TWMIL had wanted things and he had gone out and made them happen. What was my problem?

What do you want?

I want to master a handstand.

The other day I asked my mother what superpower strength

she would like to have had and she said, "being able to fight the swan."

Chapter Twenty-five

"Too many boys," TWMIL said if he didn't want to spend the night because it was busy in my house or too loud.

TWMIL renovated my garage so that I could rent the space to someone, to be more financially self-sufficient so *you can spend more time writing*. For fifteen years the garage had been a giant closet. It was how I kept the house—all 1,100 square feet of it—fairly tidy most of the time. The garage was stuffed with furniture and boxes of old toys and bags of schoolwork and maybe-will-be-used-someday things. There were also spiders. And one light bulb hanging from the ceiling.

Step one in the renovation process was getting me to clear everything out. For months chaotic stacks awaited my attention. Some decisions were made by weather. Two boxes of letters got soaked through and then molded. Letters from my grandparents, from my father, from old boyfriends. Letters my mother had written me in my various stages of away. Forty plus years of life soaked through and rotted and plopped in a giant green dumpster.

I was being dismantled.

Piles of materials littered the yard: wooden poles dragged from a wash, railroad ties, glass cube tiles, and random pieces of metal.

TWMIL amended the electricity and ran plumbing to the little building. The rickety old garage door was removed and he made barn doors. We knocked out part of a wall to install a door and part of another wall to install a window. He fenced in the front and the side and covered it. It is a lovely space.

And there it sat.

A few months after it was done, on the way to Ikea, he burst out, "You are throwing away six hundred dollars a month."

"I am not throwing it away if I never had it in the first place," I replied.

He simmered.

Where initially TWMIL had said the guesthouse was for whenever I needed it, to rent it out or for the boys or for me to be alone and write, he pushed and pushed, suggesting I contact university departments and rent it on a short-term basis to their students who were famously busy and just needed a place nearby to sleep.

My younger son was in the throes of his Troubles and the logistics of renting the space was more than I could manage.

If you just do this thing I am telling you to do, you will be less stressed.

Raad went on a road trip with his girlfriend around the western United States. They camped and stayed in hotels and visited monuments and parks and lakes. He came home and dismantled his part of their room and put his entire life into an apartment a few miles away with a friend, delighted with all this new adulthood. A couple of months into this arrangement, TWMIL and I pulled up to find an upset and very stressed Raad outside with Layth. School was in full force and he was working as a reporter and at the library in two different departments, and his roommate had decided to move out and live with his girlfriend. "I need to look for an apartment, but I don't have time and I may lose the deposit because he broke the lease, and I can't share a room with my brother."

I suggested he stay in the guest house.

"Are you sure?" he asked.

"Of course I am sure! If you find a place, great, but if not, it is yours."

You could see the relief on his face.

TWMIL told me later he didn't think that was a good idea.

I told him he had no place to say anything in this regard.

TWMIL didn't talk to me for two days.

Once the emotion of it had passed, once Raad had talked with his friend and looked around and didn't lose his deposit but did need a place quick and put his things in storage so as not to have to move everything in and out of home again, I thanked TWMIL for making it possible for both boys to be at home with enough space between them that they could both do what they needed to do without slamming into each other.

After Raad died, TWMIL told me that my having him come back home had been a bad decision, "not that it caused what happened . . ."

§♠

A hummingbird flew into TWMIL's house and couldn't figure how to get out. TWMIL opened doors and windows as far as they would go but the hummingbird couldn't find its way. TWMIL covered the mirrors so it wouldn't hurt itself and he left.

When he came home the hummingbird was gone.

§♠

I moved back into my house just before the first anniversary of Raad's death. My younger son was coming back from Colorado and TWMIL was on a trip in South America. I left behind many things in TWMIL's house. I kept thinking I would go back, not for them, but for him. I told myself I would go back when I was ready. I would go back once my younger son was settled. It's not that I stopped loving TWMIL; I felt exactly the same way I always had, only now my whole body was informing me I couldn't be near him.

I still feel this way.

I left things I hoped would let him understand that I'd be returning:

the books of distract

the drawings and notes

I-threw-myself-into-your-world-and-literally-climbed-mountains blue cargo pants, frayed at the ankles

I-am-still-young black shirt with polka dots

I-live-here sweatpants

you-are-my-person hard drive back-up for my computer

I-will-be-here-in-the-morning makeup

I-love-you Post-its on the mirrors

I-am-here-in-the-morning-and-need-shoes-to-protect-my-feet-from-the-rocks-and-dirt flip-flops

I-am-yours underwear

the red polka dot dress that was also the owl-crashing-into-the-car-on-mother's-day purchase, the what-have-you-done dress, the broken-everything and I-desperately-want-to-hold-onto-this-one-good-thing dress with spaghetti straps, the even-though-we-have-sex-in-your-friend's-cabin dress we are broken. I am broken, even in white dots, even with your hands on me.

But I didn't go back.

He put his house up for sale. He returned all of those things to me in a giant duffle bag.

Reminders of TWMIL are all over my house, in every room, in the appliances, the plumbing, the guesthouse. In every day.

Did he remember his hands all over me when he touched my things or did he just pile everything in?

There is no trace of me in his house. And now he lives in a new house where I don't exist.

"Ma, there are too many memories here," my younger son tells me in much the same way TWMIL talked about how he needed to travel, to get away. "We need to leave, Ma."

I will help you with a house, but only in Tucson because I don't know the market in Los Angeles.

I know what is best for you.

You are not capable of making decisions.

You are not enough.

We replay relationships we have struggled with until we get them right.

At the dog's urging, I step outside before dawn into the gentle damp to greet the day that keeps happening even though you're gone. The dog stands by my side. It used to bother me how her hair could be so soft and you could be dead all in the same moment. Now I see it this way:

You are the softness of her hair.

You are the cool concrete path beneath my feet, the one that connects the square of basketball court I had put in for your brother with the porch I had built so you could sit in the shade and read on the wood swing Traudi gave us that we hung next to the lemon tree.

You are the dew in the air.

You are the birds waking up.

You are the first hummingbird at the feeder.

You are the stories I tell myself to get through each day.

You are the deliciousness of my clean-sheeted bed.

You are that open road near Flagstaff where the sky stretches itself over gentle hills.

You are the smile on that pretty girl's face.

You are three yellow daisies.

You are the delicious sweet of the grapefruit I picked from our tree.

You are deep belly breaths.

You are the funny succulent that has burst forth by the front porch.

You are Wayne's well-cut clothing, his smooth leather shoes.

You are coffee-infused mascarpone cheese on Sunday.

You are blueberries.

You are a tray full of qirshalle just out of the oven.

You are musakhan on your grandmother's birthday.

You are the breeze that pushes around the branches of the pine tree.

You are the dog at the end of my bed as I write.

You are the sleek of my laptop.

You are the company of the Italians as TWMIL sobbed to them about your death.

You are the hummingbird right now at the feeder.

You are a good run.

You are Ami's offer of low maintenance company on this awful day.

You are the ridiculous mustache on the man at the gallery.

You are everything that works inside my body.

You are your brother when he is happy.

You are afternoons with Meme.

You are my person.

You are the ink that flows from my pen.

You are the pen itself.

You are our yard that is sensitive to disruption, the five tombstone roses, half the fig tree, and the tiny orange tree that died. Maybe you are also the twisted acacia that blew over the night your father moved out all those years ago.

You are the hammock hanging between the two Chilean mesquite trees.

You are writing every day.

You are gratitude when it comes.

You are moments of insight.

You are my former patient getting it together for a while.

You are not the wind or the dead leaves.

You are not my twisted gut.

You are not the cold in the floors or the rattle of the windows.

You are not terrible drivers.

You are not chipped paint or tight jeans.

You are the hummingbird that just darted by, the smile I feel forming.

You are the bright in the clouds, the blue in the sky.

You are the heat that knows just when to turn on.

You are writing in the morning.

You are no pressure.

You are the sleep I had last night.

You are quiet.

You are the courage to let go.

You are the twitter in the trees, the soft of the dog.
You are this moment and the next.

Chapter Twenty-six

The eastside mall often has an Indian blockbuster among its feature films. I went with Ami to see *War*, about an elite group within the government whose mission it is to track and destroy any threats. Hrithik Roshan's character goes off the grid and becomes close to a woman because she is the object of desire of one of the villains. In between dodging bullets and a killer dance routine, he asks her to do something for him.

"You are a loner," she tells him. "Your loyalty is to the nation and you don't know what it is like to need people, to come home to someone. I could never trust you for these reasons."

I am born from this.

I fell for this.

I was talking to TWMIL's sister about my mother's job and how I didn't find out until I was in my twenties and I was so resentful. His sister looked at me and said, "but she was doing her job by not telling you."

For my emotional survival I always had to go large. Huge. Tell everyone.

If I had been medicated at sixteen/at twenty-four/at forty . . . would there have been less struggle?

Would you still be here?

Things TWMIL said to me that became Post-it notes I wrote to my broken self

I will hold you as long as you need.

I will not demand a thing from you during this awful time however long it lasts.

I will rock you until you feel the earth's rhythm again, until the waves are in sync with yours, until the fresh grass perfumes your wrists.

I will hold you in silence until you're ready to talk.

I will hold you in wild discussion until you're ready for silence.

My home is yours.

Put your feet up.

Sleep sweet in my bed. If you wake in the night, I will hold you.

If you can't get up in the morning, I will go to work on your behalf.

I will hold you as long as you need, cook for you whenever you want, nourish you however I can.

I will be your mother, your friend, your sister; I will be your rock.

Together we will read, walk, stare at the stars, shout at the moon.

I will hold you as long as you need. You don't have to go far. Open your eyes or close them. Breathe in or breathe out.

I am here.

I've got you.

We will get through this as one.

Chapter Twenty-seven

One night while my younger son was still away and before I had moved home, I woke up to Luna's fussing. I crawled out of TWMIL's giant bed, wandered through the silent house and opened the back door for her to go out, but she wouldn't go. I gave her fresh water, but she wouldn't drink. She followed me into the guest room where I settled under the covers to read. For the next hour or two, Luna was up and down. She came to the side of the bed as though she needed something, but she wouldn't go out and nothing seemed to satisfy her. She was so fussed that at one point I lay down on the floor next to her and rubbed her belly and talked to her. Finally, in the wee hours of the morning, I led her outside and walked with her into the dark. It turned out that her bother was a giant need to shit that was not quite as large as her newly developed reluctance to go outside alone at night.

I slept shortly before five and when I woke at seven thirty I made the bed for the first time in days and opened all the curtains. Luna and I set out for our long walk around the neighborhood, and as we rounded the corner by a tiny church (one of four in walking distance of TWMIL's house) whose marquee read *no more excuses, move forward* I felt as though a burden had been lifted, as though I was the one who had taken a giant shit during the witching hours.

I asked Luna if she had taken my burdens the night before when I was comforting her and a hawk flew out of one of the tiny trimmed oleander bushes and swooped by me at eye level.

If I had extended my arm, I could have touched it.

§.

TWMIL was setting out to explore beaches in Mexico and wanted me to join him. He was frustrated that I said no, again, and that I wanted time on my own. He said that I was too much in my head, that I thought too much. I told him *someone has to.*

I woke up alone just after four in the massive bed. After stretching I went into the narrow yellow kitchen that I'd spent days mopping, tidying, cleaning, but not cooking in. I poured milk for Nescafé into the blue mug Raad received on orientation day when he started university. The dog needed to pee, so I put on my outside shoes and we wandered around the weed-filled yard.

This was one of my other intentions for while TWMIL was away: to weed the house, perhaps a controlled burn; the dead-everywhere grass was depressing. Instead of *doing things*, I hung out with my thoughts, read, wrote, danced, walked the dog. I made popcorn, watched an entire season of *Broadchurch*. I even took a bath. It was fucking glorious.

After the dog peed and we came back inside, I leaned down to pick up her bowl so I could give her fresh water. There was a moth floating spread-eagle, probably the same moth that had been flitting around the night before keeping me company while I cleaned. I dipped my fingers in the water and scooped it out, then refilled and returned the water bowl to its place. I felt the moth's wet wings rest against my skin and its legs begin to wiggle. It stood up and shook off the water with the movement of a larger animal.

I tried to put it on a dish towel, but it jumped to another finger as though it had not almost drowned but instead had chosen to go for a swim and was now exhilarated and wanted to play.

I didn't heat my milk on the stove the way I used to. Instead, I stuck it in the microwave, as though I was in some kind of a hurry. Just before boiling, I pulled it out and mixed in a heaping spoon of Nescafé while the weightless, tan moth sat on the index finger of my left hand. I tried again to put it on the towel, but it flew onto my pajamas.

We returned to the darkened bedroom over-filled with the king-sized bed that was like its own country and that I wanted to love. The moth, the dog, and I settled back among the pillows.

※

Later, Luna and I walked side by side, her leash slack because she has reached that age where she is easy company unless there's a cat.

That far corner of TWMIL's neighborhood is a thruway for people without homes or in some sort of transition. The park is on one side of the neighborhood and Stone Avenue is just down the way.

A man staggered out of the wash and walked toward us.

"Who's walking who?" he asked.

"We are walking together," I responded, smiling, because accuracy matters, even with a drunk person who is just making conversation.

You are so literal.

A Jack Russell investigated the dried grasses on the corner of Seventh and Lester. Both of us saw him a block ahead. I wondered aloud whether it was the same dog who charged across a yard toward us in wild barking a few weeks earlier, or if it was Kelly, who we would see at the park. Luna tensed but we kept walking. "What do you think he's up to?" I asked her.

A few feet away now, the dog bounded over out of the tall dead grass and Luna was disarmed by his cheeriness. They sniffed each other, a darling mix of tall and short, eager and tentative. The Jack Russell played with her ears and then dropped back to greet me. This back and forth repeated as we continued our walk north on Seventh.

"Is this your dog?" I asked the man working on a car in his driveway.

He shook his head

"Is this your dog?" I asked the woman who pulled up in a small yellow car. Her hair was pulled back and she looked to be in a hurry. She shook her head. A man from the house called to her. He came out and said that he saw this dog every morning walking itself, had no idea where it came from or who its owner was, "but it sure is nice." He leaned down to pat it and picked up a rolled-up, used mini pad that was on the ground nearby and dropped it in the trashcan.

Luna and I kept walking north with our new companion bobbing along beside us.

"Do you know whose dog this is?" I asked a scruffy man in black clothes who passed us on his bike.

"I sure don't," he said. "He is cute. If I didn't have two at home, I'd take him with me. Kills me to see how people are with their dogs." He kept riding. A giant finial was welded to the back of his bike.

The dog snaked a trail behind us and both Luna and I relaxed in his easy company.

"That dog is so smart just following you like that," said a large cheery man who was backing out of a mechanic's shop in a lowrider that *you would have admired if you were here.*

A junkyard holds down the northwest corner of Seventh and Flores. Its chain-linked rusted sadness looks like a place they show *in the kind of movies you like* where things have not gone well for anyone. The Jack Russell sniffed at the thick dead grasses. The old gray pit bull mix who lives there worked the perimeter.

At Seventh and Rillito the Jack Russell was gone. Both Luna and I kept turning around to look for him.

#1 Pho is just around the corner, as is the spot where a man with a mental illness was shot dead by police after his family requested they do a welfare check.

I think you loved #1 Pho with its spacious seating in red vinyl booths as much for the food as for the seediness of the neighborhood where it is located.

My neighborhood.

Raad's soul and body were on different timetables, a weird inverse of Middle Eastern Standard Time, where he was living two or three or four speed-years for every one of ours.

When he was three, his father said that by five, he'd be more mature than both of us.

We teased him for being eighty as he watched old movies with the volume at sixty.

When Noreen first met him—he was four—she said to John, "this kid is forty-five."

In the obituary that I still haven't written, instead of saying twenty-one and two months, I will say eighty-four. This would explain his wisdom and how he managed to see so many movies in such a short lifetime. And why he and my mother were completely in sync.

✿

I thought I was doing all the right things: fruits and vegetables on the table, organic when I could afford it, private school, charter school—even though both concepts offended me—right school, white school, nurtured my boys into American dreaming only to have one killed the other dive into a darker world, surface, and swim away with his demons for a time.

We gave them a cozy house, wooden toys, books—so many damn books—regular bedtime, routine, chores, allowances, pets, stories before sleep (including the first five Harry Potter novels read aloud in a variety of British accents), vacations to the beach, visits to Ireland, Palestine, and Jordan, family albums. I cuddled them, read to them, loved and fed them, created safe and happy, created space for joy.

And then it was gone and I found myself dead inside with no better-around-the-corner. I held onto my surviving boy with such a rough grip he ran further.

A part of me yearned for the sidekick role, antidote to the hard and sad. I wanted to lie down on the tracks of the nightly beer-drinking train.

I went along went along went along.

I woke up in TWMIL's giant bed hating the life I was living.

Beer, pizza, and bicycles; that's what good friends are made of, TWMIL sent this card to a friend, sealed it with hot wax. My heart folded in on itself, the aftermath of drinking too much and standing in a place not my own. This kind of lightness would never make sense to me.

Maybe you are not meant to live a normal life, he told me more than once.

There was no going back, forward carried so much pain, and yet the dog was still soft and sweet, two jobs awaited me. I still had a son and a mother and friends.

Sadness is two bags of groceries, not five.

Sadness is pulling up to the house and carrying those two bags in alone because my older boy is dead and my younger son is away.

Sadness is now.

Chapter Twenty-eight

"Crashed" I texted my younger son as I pulled up in front of our house in Raad's truck.

Earlier he had asked me to pick him up from a girl's house and while we were on our way home he said he needed to stop by his friend's house and over the next few blocks it became apparent that he had asked me to pick him up so I could drive him to his friend's house and leave him there.

At ten o'clock at night.

This after blowing off a doctor's appointment.

This after an argument during which he had gotten out of the car while we were stopped at an intersection. I had managed to convince him to get back in because he was clearly high and we were across from the police station.

We got to his friend's house and I threatened to go inside, but I didn't follow through because his energy was bad and he'd not slept. To say he was not himself is an understatement and so I screamed into the night as I drove and I imagined driving into a pole, a tree, a building, anything that would hurt and thud and make the worry stop. I floored it. Fortunately, Gloria was an older truck and by the time she had accelerated, I had moved my foot to the left.

This was why when I pulled up in front of our sweet little house, I texted that one word. *Crashed.*

Into a wall, into hatred, the end, revulsion, it is all true, but not the way he thinks.

"Where?" he texted me a few minutes later.

I did not answer.

⁊

Raad had worked at the car wash of a dealership the semester before he graduated high school. He had to be there at six o'clock in the morning and sometimes took the bus across town when it was still dark outside; sometimes I'd drive him. He carried a knife and prided himself on being able to handle the heat and the work.

They hired a huge man who had just moved from Michigan. Raad said that he was nice but also a little scary and had an edge to him. A couple of days a week, a nameless Mexican food truck would park on the road near the dealership and sell excellent burritos. One day Raad's new coworker saw the *open* sign and said with the excitement of a young child, "Hey look! Abierto's is here again!"

Raad could not tell the story without laughing.

He no longer found this man to be scary.

TWMIL called to say that when he was driving back from a town north of here, he neared the spot of Raad's accident and he began talking to him, had asked aloud if Raad had been a "dumb, unco-ordinated drunk kid who misjudged things or . . ." just as he said this, the full can of tea that he had wedged in the backseat flew up and hit him on the head.

"There's your answer," he told me. "He didn't do it on purpose."

I can tell you exactly what happened. The driver wasn't paying attention. It was night and he was driving too fast and probably in the fast lane. He didn't expect to see him there and by the time he did, there was nothing he could have done.

As I type this there is a funny noise at my window. It is early morning and the curtains are closed against the brightness. I lean over and pull the curtain aside. A baby dove stands on the window ledge. The mother is standing in their nest on the top of the basketball net my younger son and I had assembled when their father first moved out. She's watching her baby, keeping an eye for predators.

Chapter Twenty-nine

The first night I took Zoloft, more than a year After, I woke up at 1:44 to my brain rearranging itself. Thoughts lay by the wayside for inspection. The traffic jams that had loaded my mind for years, the sentences that couldn't find their way from beginning to end, were free to relocate. I envisioned pathways in my head moving smoothly with no accidents to report.

That night I joined America, officially medicated against the mess and stress of life.

The next morning, I could see the day's details without emotion or extra thought. I felt the burning hot of my coffee cup and noticed the hair ties piled on the table, the glasses stacked in the kitchen, all without any additional commentary. Instant mindfulness. The antidepressant aspect of the medication would not affect my mind for weeks, but a shift was happening in my brain.

On the third day of taking Zoloft, I had sweaty feet and was so tired I was calm.

"Zoloft had me drooling in the corner," a friend told me. "I stopped after a couple of days."

Even as I will never know what happened that night, I know you are at peace.

On the fifth day of taking the medicine I lost all desire to express myself in writing.

Did we both lose ourselves to our fantasy of America?

After a week on Zoloft, I had lost all urgent thinking, probably because I was almost comatose for half the day.

My writing brain had left the building.

Ten days in and I was sleeping eight to ten hours a day and experiencing no emotions, no ideas. The dove on the porch swing that two weeks prior would have swelled my heart with the awareness that Raad was nearby, was now just a dove on the porch swing.

Things fell into place, slowed down, and eased up. My interactions with my younger son were happier and my interactions with TWMIL were fewer, as though he too were a drug and with Zoloft's help, I was titrating down.

Four weeks into the medication and I lost the compulsive need to write that I have had since I was a child. No stories. No poems. No ruminating.

I could be functional and busy and completely disconnected in a fabulous Pollyanna sort of way. *I'm fine. Everything's fine.* I was truly American.

More than a month into the medication, I slept so much that my bones softened. I had no feelings as I watched the faraway action of my life through a thick chunk of glass, like watching drawings go about their business.

Before and After, I lived years of demon-tired as my younger son coped with/escaped from life by trying to burn out his brain. I was in a constant tug-of-war between being relieved he was home and not too skinny and the rage at his swagger in the face of my worried exhaustion.

Two parents can offer opposing messages. One can say, "I'm glad you're home safe," while the other one can rage "how dare you sneak out after everything that's happened? You left the door unlocked! You left the gate open! The dogs could have gotten out! You are behaving so selfishly!"

These things can't be conveyed by one person in a way that makes sense to the using brain that is only absorbing the emotion. In that scenario, the emotions from the one parent are in conflict and the using brain will always respond to the larger emotion and not hear any of the words. When my younger son stepped out of a gold Kia SUV at seven one morning and said, "That's my Uber driver," I could barely look at him. He greeted the dog sweetly (a good sign!) and I turned away and walked back in the house exhausted again because I had been awake since four when I found the front door open and unlocked. I flipped over the worry and sadness for a few hours alone. Alone because I'd run out of resources. No one wants to hear the story anymore.

"Do something about it," everyone seemed to say.

No matter how many times I'd *done something about it*, he still struggled. I had to stand strong until he was able to work through it.

"Just love him," Traudi told me countless times. "That's all you can do."

Later, after I'd run and showered and eaten and been able to think myself off the ledge while he slept, I regretted my ugly and wanted to replay his return home and tell him how much I loved him and how thankful I was that he was safe.

This is another of the fuck-all that one dead son offers you. You micromanage your every breath with your living son for fear that you might say the wrong thing and those will be the last words he ever hears from you.

Things got bad again—not as bad as they had been Before but headed in that direction.

And then my younger son agreed to go to detox.

I dropped him off and prayed that twenty-three hours around vomiting misery would knock some sense into him.

My words were dried up, dead leaves in my head, swept away by Zoloft.

❧

I was writing about TWMIL *do you know why we aren't married?* and thinking, this is not what I want to write about, when I heard a series of taps. I looked up and there was a tiny bird hopping on the wood trim that holds up my window, pecking for food in the worn-out spaces.

Even on meds, even not feeling much in the way of emotion, I could spot this as Raad reminding me again, as he does, that he was there with me and to keep going, just like another day at the park when two vermillion flycatchers collided at the moment I came to the decision to go back full-on to trying to get my stories published.

The white butterfly, the contrails, the headstand, there were signs everywhere.

This is why we are not married.

Now that you are gone, who will go to the bookstores and find my books and turn them out so they are prominently displayed?

Chapter Thirty

I met a woman whose daughter had died at sixteen in a motorcycle accident. She said that she didn't want to take medications or use drugs or alcohol because she needed to feel everything to get through it. I thought I could manage that approach but more than a year After and I would find myself on the kitchen floor or being at work and not being able to form words.

With Zoloft, I spent the day busy with gentle chores. I filled the bird feeders with seeds. I made the sugar water mixture for the hummingbirds and when it cooled, I brought in the empty feeder and cleaned it out. I refilled it and went outside to hang it from the mesquite tree in front of my window. A very fat hummingbird flew right up and drank, inches from my face.

I felt nothing.

One time I ran into this woman when I was with TWMIL and when he was out of earshot, she told me that she had gone on a date with him a long time ago. I was not surprised, partly because Tucson is small that way, but also because *it's all about the connections.* Just as the cop had one dead stepson and he carried that darkness into our knowing, just like the woman who sold us Luna would turn out to have one dead son, we are all nails in this wooden board with rubber bands wrapping around our necks figuring us into all kinds of crazy patterns.

Lost: unable to find something; unable to orient oneself to location; without hope in the world.

Exiled: forced to inhabit another place.

Those were my words from Before, when I knew loss in a middle-class, immigrant sort of way, loss with safety nets and savings accounts and angst and sad and semi-impossible but potentially poetic stories.

The real loss of a marriage, a best friend, a firstborn son, nearly a second son, hope . . . there were no names for these new spaces I occupied.

I took medicine to stop the crying, to defog the brain, to keep from spending the afternoon on the kitchen floor.

I broke up with TWMIL and felt relief and no longer wanted to watch my head explode.

I chose sleep over creating.

During the time that I was teaching creative writing at the VA, I came up with an exercise that was ostensibly about observation but was actually about mindfulness and shifting your thinking and your sense of self.

Here it is:

Write *I accept* and describe your surroundings.

Example:

I accept this table.

I accept that it is cool underneath my hands.

I accept the light in the room won't turn off.

I accept that there are four people in the room.

With time, I would turn the attention to the self.

Example:

I accept my hand.

I accept the brown and the wrinkled and the chipped nail polish.

I accept the swollen pinkie finger.

I accept that there is pain in the pinkie finger.

I accept that I don't like the pain.

I accept that the pain makes me feel slow and old.

When my students did these exercises, over time there would be a shift in how they saw things, how they saw themselves. There would be moments of acceptance. Sometimes those moments extended.

I was describing this to the doctor I work for and she was intrigued. "Where did you learn that?" she asked.

"I made it up," I told her.

She smiled and made a humph noise in a way that indicated to me that she was impressed, and for the first time in a while, I felt a bump of pride.

There were strings of days when the only writing I did involved these statements.

I accept that I would like to blossom.

I accept that I get in my own way.

I accept that when I take the full dose of the medication I can navigate things better, even if I have gained ten pounds and I feel no emotions.

"It's all a trade-off," another doctor I worked for told me.

As a young girl I thought my long neck, long legs, and long hair were the required tickets, along with regular practice that would make me a great ballerina. I didn't understand that a lack of coordination, the consistent challenge my brain finds to get my arms and legs to follow steps, might get in the way.

Your form is vital to balancing your handstand. Your core must be engaged: back straight, butt in, arms by your ears as you push up through your shoulders, toes pointed, both for aesthetics and to lift you up closer to the sky.

If you're having a hard time pushing up, work on your upper body strength.

Chapter Thirty-one

My younger son blew blood from his nose into paper towels because his cocaine use was fucking up his sinuses.

We sat in the public mental health clinic for an appointment that he set up for himself (another good sign!), and a woman asked me if he was my only one.

"No," I replied. "But he is the baby."

"How many others do you have?" she asked.

"Four."

"Wow," the woman said.

Dangerous to lie when your memory is terrible, I learned in my early twenties when I told people that my father was dead.

I am both an incredibly honest person and a total liar.

My every breath is a paradox.

Balance.

Balance can mean inertia, stasis. An unoccupied seesaw. Do I need other people to get momentum?

Lying was my new truth.

Lying has always been my truth.

It started with saying "fine" whenever someone asked how I was. And then giving updates on Raad as though he were alive. And my younger son as though things were sailing along smoothly for him. I could justify both of these morally. It didn't take long, however, before my truths were fewer and further between.

Are you married?

Yes.

Where are you from?

California.

What do you do for a living?

Private investigator.

For real?

For real.

It got easier and easier. The more I did it, the deeper down my real self settled. I didn't realize I was building walls, that the one thing I had prided myself on was leaving the building. By the time I realized, I was in too deep.

Was it the medication that allowed me to lie without guilt?

Truth had been my currency, my anchor, and suddenly I was free-falling with no wing, no reserve, no superhero to swoop me up.

And it was glorious.

✿

I watch the women around me age in a way I too must be aging. They thicken and shrivel and gray so gradually that you'd only notice if you didn't see them too often.

That one walks out of the building. Her stooped shoulders and clenched grip on her bag announce for miles that she is not happy, but she is glad to be leaving. She is older than me by a few years, but since in my mind's view of myself I am in my twenties, she looks decades older. Her clothes have been the same in all the years I have known her. I tell myself I am saving money and the environment by shopping secondhand, but I have probably gone through a literal ton of apparel while she owns only a small suit-case.

I mention this aging thing to a younger coworker whose mother died when she was a child and whose father is two years my junior. I say I am going to wear braids until I am 105. She says, "Black don't crack," and I feel a sense of pride.

Twice I have been asked to work with older patients who "want someone not so green and closer to their own age." I'm not sure when I fell into that category.

"You could be my sister," another younger coworker says.

I could be her mother.

Her mother is also dead.

My only goal is to master a handstand.

Chapter Thirty-two

Boundaries.

"You have none," says my walled-up mother whose closest friends don't know her truth. She cites my inviting our mailman in for breakfast as an example. In her mind this is incomprehensible and therefore a flaw.

If there is inherited trauma, can there not be inherited hospitality? Inherited warmth? The need for close human interaction? I am only half from my mother after all. Seems to me that inviting someone you consider a friend in for breakfast is simply a human thing to do.

"How are you friends with your mailman?"

Clarence has come to my house every day for the past eighteen years and we talk for hours; of course he is my friend.

I have no boundaries and I have all the boundaries. My boundaries are misplaced and no longer serve me: a white picket fence around a castle. An alligator-filled moat around a tent. Concertina wire around an open field. Not in sync and not the right materials.

My mother has said things to me that should have stayed thoughts, words that tried to become self-fulfilling prophecies:

"Don't ever sing to your children because you have a voice that will make them run away."

"You shouldn't work for anyone; you've too much of an authority problem."

"No man will ever be strong enough to handle you."

Both my mother and TWMIL have lived surface lives of great adventure. I wormed my way into their hearts, broke down their walls, and sat closer to both of them than they were to anyone else. And they each resented the other.

And then Raad died and I could offer neither of them any form of emotional sustenance.

Neither could bear to see me hurt.

Neither could tolerate the other.

If I got closer to either one, the other was unhappy and let me know.

My once-closest friend had a similar tug-of-war with her husband and mother; her husband won and yanked her out of the dance away from all of us.

❧

"Let no man put weights on you, not even your sons," I wrote following a lonely birthday after my younger son had been returned by his father and questioned by the police twice in as many weeks while TWMIL was gone to play in Mexico.

This statement was followed by pages and pages of affirmations and encouragement.

The crazy in me is a like a secret sister tucked away in the attic. When everyone is miles away and frolicking, storms shake the house and my secret sister comes wailing, twitching, talking, banging doors, kicking, throwing glass. People keep their distance, never really seeing her because on the calm, sunny days when they are around, everything seems just right.

"I want to be with a man stronger than everything," I wrote. "Stronger than my problems, stronger than my worries."

That kind of strong can knock your dreams clear off the playing field.

Careful what you wish for.

Destruction is wrought by men on those around them, be it kitchen cabinets or soft skin, so much force and power with nowhere to put it except objects owned by women and women themselves.

Mother Earth, for example.

In the few months before I met TWMIL, I could feel the sea change, the shifting of the tectonic plates that slid us into one another. We had both been given information about the other before we met and were primed and at the tippy end of our high-rise diving boards ready to jump. He was used to the literal jumps and I was schooled in the metaphoric ones. He caught me midair and held me there for years as we did glorious flips and floats. And then an owl swooped down and tried to grab me . . . or that's what the white man who loved me thought. The owl was actually issuing a warning that the pool had been drained and we were just about to . . . three days later my older son was hit by a 58,000-pound truck while he was alone on a highway in the middle of the night.

During those years we were soaring, the white man who loved me held all of my backpacks, the one that held my younger son, the one that held my work, the one that held my house, and the one that held my responsibilities, even the one that held my dog. I didn't think I could carry them all by myself and he was superhero strong. If I had held onto them while we were soaring, would our balance have been better? Would we not have crashed? (Would he have let me carry them?)

I am on my feet again. My knees hurt and my neck and shoulders ache, but I am building my core and carrying all the damn backpacks.

I spent years following signs, walking square into what I thought I wanted until everything that mattered got taken away or bruised. Both my beginning and ending with him were written, a physical force that pushed and pulled.

I still miss him, still love him, still can't be with him.

TWMIL and my mother are opposites. And they are twins.

The self-help masters say that you recreate issues that you never worked through and you will keep recreating them until you get them right.

Patterns of impossible men who obscure vulnerability.

My mother started this trend, found a man who could never be hers and regurgitated the vocabulary to tell me TWMIL could never be mine, nor I his, not really.

I was talking to Dr. K about these threads that connect everything. I told her how I thought I had chopped them all off, but this umbilical cord is still going strong, made of steel and over half a century old.

"Could you try drawing what that looks like?" she asked me.

My judgy voice whispered what a dumb idea that was.

And then I went home and drew two stick figures. My mother's ropes all sprung from her head, but they reached me everywhere and multiplied in a tangle. And while there was one very strong rope connecting our hearts, there were a million tendrils of judgment, responsibility, and thought. What to think. What to like. What to eat. What to wear. Who to love. I lived a life caught in a tangle of umbilical demands.

Of course I thought I wouldn't be able to carry all my backpacks!

A couple of sessions later I came to realize that it was not so much that she imposed her thinking on me as she thought this way and didn't understand why I didn't. Where for all my life I had internalized her approach as relentless judgment, it was just who she is in the world. We were both just trying to survive.

I accept this bed.

I accept the dog lying at my feet.

I accept the sunshine coming through my window.

I accept the bite of the cold.

I accept my mother.

Chapter Thirty-three

After the memorial, people came to our house to eat plates of delicious food cooked by a Syrian woman and laid out across tables by my children's honorary aunties.

It does not feel okay to notice that food is delicious when your older son is dead.

My house overflowed with love and bursts of laughter.

A friend thought the tureen of garlic sauce was vanilla pudding.

An acquaintance told Houri that "they find kidnapped children in Disneyland by their shoes; baby stealers don't have time to swap them out."

Victoria wore a black dress and pink Converse. Note to self: this is the best funeral outfit ever.

With sweaty hands, one of Raad's coworkers handed me a gigantic bouquet of white flowers, leading my friends to speculate that he liked older women.

My backyard was filled with people of many religions, sexual orientations, backgrounds, races, and ages, all laughing or crying or telling stories.

For the last time, my home became again what it had once been: joyous.

I have never liked the color yellow. It is painful and scratchy to look at.

After Raad died, however, yellow showed up in flowers.

Emily, a girl he had known since middle school, brought me a bouquet of wild yellow flowers on the day of the memorial. They lasted four weeks. I began noticing yellow flowers all over the place, as did she. Raad had given me a pot of yellow flowers for my birthday the year before and I planted them by the front steps. They, too, died. Tiny red berries replaced them.

Every yellow flower is a soul's reminder.

🔊

TWMIL enjoyed going out for a beer.

I got into the rhythm of it and I liked the buzz of strong, dark beer.

I'd find myself in one bar or another and about halfway into the first drink, I didn't care how shallow I'd become. It was an easy happy, a sweet antidote to my life of complex and heartbreaking stories.

And then I couldn't stand it and felt like I was wasting my time and losing myself.

I missed him though. His love, his warmth, his cheeriness.

Because I could no longer be *all in*, I kept my distance.

I taught myself handstands.

How I feel after a handstand is glorious.

Chapter Thirty-four

Luna and I were walking down an alley when I caught sight of movement behind a fence.

We backtracked.

Through the rusted metal slats that had been woven into a chain link fence, a ratty white goat covered in clumps of dirty dreads stared back at me. A few feet away stood a smaller goat, neater and with a giant belly.

We stood staring at each other for a bit and then left.

The next day Luna and I returned. This time the goats came up to the fence. Luna stuck her nose through a space at the bottom. The male goat did the same. They both snorted and stepped back.

For weeks, stopping at the goat yard was part of our routine.

One morning we stopped and there were two awkward, black-booted kids that tumbled around the prickly grasses.

Each day the babies changed noticeably, bigger or sturdier or with stronger colors to their coats.

The ram's rear was encrusted with poop and hemorrhoids. They were both dirty, dirtier than is normal for a farm animal. The mother goat had mud on her knees.

I once had a client who had been abused, sex-trafficked, and was emotionally very young. I was driving her somewhere when we saw a girl walking down the street with dirt on the knees of her jeans. "That girl been on her knees giving blow jobs is why she has those marks; that mark stays forever."

Time marches by in pages and pages and pages, day after day after sleepless night after day of encouragement and reminders to *do yoga* and *walk the dog* and *rise above* and *find the beauty* and treat my younger son with compassion and not let him define me and the feeling of free-falling in a vortex of self-blame.

Sweet chickadee, this world has fucked with you something fierce.

When tragedy rolls up in its shiny Escalade, you can't help looking behind you. "What the fuck did I do wrong?" you will ask eventually unless you are God-oriented and then you will tell yourself there is a plan involved. It might take you a minute, you might be mad at God, not on speaking terms for a bit, but belief is belief and you'll be back riding through the village like a new bride before you know it.

Medicated exhaustion is my full-body Kevlar. Nothing gets in.

Antidepressants are life's condom.

Can I lay me down to sleep and start the fuck over?

My beautiful boys grew up in a sweet house soaked in love. I loved them more than I knew was possible to love another human.

How the fuck could this happen?

I've written my story a hundred ways and can't ever get it right. White lies. Fifty-one percent Western Asian/North African. My battles are balanced. Theft. Forbidden love. Colonialism. All of that lives inside me. The jig is up. Can't trust what you can't hold.

Ours was supposed to be the dream immigrant story.

Am I an immigrant? A refugee?

To tell my story honestly is to speak secrets and share intimacies. My public is private.

I thought I made my peace long ago with fiction being the emergency exit from my impossible circumstances.

And then my husband wouldn't touch me.

And then my father died.

And then my younger son got a taste for the dark side.

And then my best friend vanished.

And then my older son died.

Died sounds like a gentle act. Breathe in, breathe out, and then you are gone. His dying was not gentle and parts of him went scattered for miles during the witching hours.

Sweet chickadee, the world is still fucking with you.

Chapter Thirty-five

I am selfish with my younger son sometimes.

As a mother, I was always very what-is-mine-is-yours.

Until the Troubles.

Until the book of poetry that contained the *you've got the chops* promise scribbled on a green index card got sold for pennies.

One morning I took a shower after another terrible night. I lifted the bottle of fancy conditioner that I had bought for myself as a treat because while everything is going to shit at least you can have soft hair. Maybe he felt the same way: the bottle was empty.

Everything that was wrong in the world narrowed into that empty bottle of conditioner. I screamed and yelled and cursed and threw the bottle at the door. Because it was all of everything, in a definable, tangible, hurtable form.

Now, when he asks to use my lotion, the threads that are looped around my organs and attached to those memories get yanked.

TWMIL was mostly frugal, but also incredibly generous with me. He bought me things (so many jackets, a laptop), gave me things (appliances), did things for me (pulled my younger son out of drug dens, replumbed my house, renovated my garage), and took me places (camping, whale watching, Mexico, Italy). I did not ask for these things nor did I ever take advantage of his generosity. In the years Before, I reciprocated wherever possible, though we did joke that I owed him 2,073 meals. Even as I tried to reciprocate, my seesaw was off balance. I was riding *chueca*.

After, my attitude changed. I became particular about things even when they didn't matter to me. I made sure I got my cup back rather than leaving it at his house, for example, even though I really didn't care about the cup. *This is my thing and I don't want to lose it.* Over a year after we had been apart, TWMIL still had a picture of him with my dog on his social media page, and while they had adored each other, it bothered me.

During my post-divorce series of unfortunate choices, the man who wore swim trunks wanted to move in a week after meeting. He did not move in, but I probably let him get too close.

"That makes me prickly," I'd say about things that annoyed me.

"*Prickly* is a great expression," he said.

When I suspected he was cheating, I googled his username and found him on two dating sites. On one of his profiles he talked about needing to get a lot of exercise, "otherwise I get prickly." This commandeering of my word in order to improve his cheating options bothered me as much as the cheating and lying.

If this commandeering of another's self is the root of white male privilege, does that mean white male privilege is an issue of boundaries?

Appropriation: taking something for one's own use without permission.

I live near the university, which means people are always parking on our street and riding their bikes or walking to campus. Sometimes it annoys me and sometimes it doesn't. There was a time—before my divorce when things were particularly stressful—when it made me furious. There was a time—not long before his death—when it enraged Raad.

"Rats, when there are too many in a cage, become aggressive," my mother said. While true, this struck me as an odd analogy.

A man lived down the street with his sister and her family. There were always plastic bins full of empty Budweiser cans in front of their house and several veteran and military stickers on his car.

I came home one day many years ago to find cars in front of my house. I parked up the street in the shade of their orange trees (now deceased), a nice respite as it was late spring and the days had gotten sunny and warm.

My younger son, who was three, and I walked out of the house a short while later to find him writing down the license of the truck in front of our house.

"Is this yours?" he asked.

"No, it belongs to his gardener," I said, pointing toward my next-door neighbor's house.

"You parked in front of my house," he said. His face was a ruddy pink.

"I parked on the street where there was space," I replied.

"You have a space behind your house where you could park," he said.

"It is not your business to tell me where to park," I replied.

He pointed at my trees that I had only recently realized had been off the irrigation and looked sparse, as though they were dying (they are still alive). "You are a terrible neighbor," he said. "Not taking care of your trees."

"Speaking of terrible neighbors," I replied, my younger son's tiny hand in mine. "We have ridden past you on bikes so many times and said good morning and you never respond."

"I didn't know you spoke English," he said.

"So, it's like that," Clarence would later say when I told him this story about the man we all came to refer to as Mr. Happiness.

In the intervening years I have seen him so drunk he's peed himself. I have seen him stand and stare at us without saying hello.

TWMIL made a point of talking to him—"He's a decent guy. Harmless. Veteran."—after which he offered my younger son a job doing yardwork.

Less than a year after I met TWMIL, a man in North Carolina killed three young Arab Americans, supposedly over parking issues.

TWMIL also talked to the college boys who rented the house across the street, the one with the Confederate flag covering a wall of their living room that you could see from my front porch.

"They're just kids," TWMIL said.

I have to remind myself of these stories on the days when I find myself missing TWMIL.

I have to remember that he took the cop's side after Sandra Bland died.

I will light you up.

I get a glimpse of something through the parting in the front curtain that the dog made when she was barking earlier. It looks like a giant cardboard box, but it turns out to be the door of my car with sun hitting it at an angle that changes the color from white to beige.

That is how life is. You look at it from a certain angle and you are in love and then you look at it from another angle and you are being manipulated.

And then you take antidepressants and you can look everything dead-on and it's just the door of your car or a man smiling at you.

Before and after the medicine, the gravel men mattered, their scratch and weight informed me. On medication, I don't need dopamine boosts from those bad and broken and emotionally distant or rogue detectives and semi-reformed hitmen that every country has on Netflix: Luther and Sartaj and Bob and Hector and Jhon and William and Cormac.

They are the down-south singers who walk a line between insightful and racist misogynists. Or cross the line.

They are the occasional desperate customer or client or patient.

They are the maintenance men who look too long, who test the waters because they already have access. "I was working on the roof and watching you while you were swimming and a bird clocked me on the head," Nick told me one morning. "That was your son saying don't watch my mama. Girl, you weren't kidding about the birds."

They are serrated by trauma and decorated with rough.

They know what they want and what they don't. There is no bullshit. They are the ultimate practitioners of mindfulness.

They have no boundaries and they have all the boundaries.

Gravel men are a safe kind of dangerous, or just plain dangerous. In my post-divorce fountain of overwhelm, they had been home plate. For the little over a year that I was medicated, they held no appeal.

This is the fat to skim off my boiling combination of 50.7/49.3.

When I had to ride the subway alone at night, I would find the biggest, toughest looking man, tell him I was frightened to be there alone, and ask if I could stand with him.

Chapter Thirty-six

On medication things were what they were.

I soaked up unexpected moments of grace without attributing meaning or stories.

I drove to Phoenix with Luna in Raad's truck and bought a cast-iron chiminea covered in dragonflies from a man named Waylon.

We stopped in a field so she could pee and there were hummingbirds all over the place.

I was in the ER on my younger son's nineteenth birthday. I had been fine and then I had vomited a handful of blood for reasons that would not ever be figured out.

The tired Filipina nurse held my hair while I puked.

My younger son left work and came and stayed with me.

This was a turning point for him, when he started to shed old ways and truly fight to heal himself.

"You have to create ten shitty things for every one good thing. You don't get the good one without having gone through the shitty ones," Pam said years ago when we were talking about the work involved in art and writing.

Chapter Thirty-seven

"Someone told me it would take a year to get over the rawness of it," my mother said in reference to Raad's death. "After two years I can talk about him." She teared up. "But not much."

I am medicated so I can talk about him.

I am broken so I am medicated so I can talk about him. To him. *The last few days in particular, you have felt very close.* I smoked weed last night and could not wake up early the way I usually do.

My beer of choice has 8.5 percent alcohol and 273 calories. Drinking one of these beers is like having a meal with a friend.

For four years I drank beer with the white man who loved me, not seeing that some part of me was being siphoned away while sitting on that couch or chair or bench or barstool. I thought I was living a normal life. I was neither white nor brown. I was a person drinking a beer with the man I loved. I erased history over one beer and then another.

"Do you know why we aren't married?" TWMIL asked me when we were closer to the end than he realized. I could think of several responses, including the obvious two, that he had never asked and that I did not want to be married.

We were in a bar having a beer.

We had had another unpleasant conversation in this bar some months prior when we had gone there to meet his sister. I had said I'd drive because I had to pick my younger son up from his counseling afterwards and TWMIL had said that we wouldn't stay that long and that he would drive. And then he ordered a second beer a few minutes before when we would have to leave to be on time and said that he wanted to finish it.

"He'll be fine if you aren't there the minute it ends," he told me.

"We need to leave now," I said.

I was never late for picking up my kids nor were they ever late for school, which felt like a major accomplishment because I am late for most everything else. "How do you manage to be employed?" Raad would ask me when I'd be in the house getting ready at 9:58 when I had to be at work at ten.

I insisted and we left and ended up sitting in silence in the parking lot of the counseling place. A silence that continued for another two days.

"We are not married because you have trust issues. You don't trust enough."

"Of course I don't trust enough," I replied, not for the first time.

I was a week into medication and absent of emotions.

"Why the fuck would I?" I am sure I repeated that I trusted him as much as I trusted anyone, that I had let him further in than I had let any man before. This was true but apparently not enough.

Maybe people project that which is theirs.

Maybe I don't trust people who are not trustworthy.

Maybe I need to trust myself to know that.

He raised his voice and talked about not wanting to be *normal*. I could feel the potential for serious escalation in the same way my younger son used to pick fights so that he could access the huge emotions he was feeling but didn't know what to do with.

I stopped him. "This right now, what you are doing, this is *normal*. We are better than this." I got up, leaned over and kissed him, told him I loved him, and left.

And I felt powerful in the same way I did telling my date he didn't make me feel amazing all those years Before.

Shortly after I met TWMIL, I met an interesting woman who had written a book that I read in one sitting and enjoyed very much. And then I took her book and threw it in the giant green alley dumpster because I knew TWMIL would fall in love with her if he were to meet her.

Is that craziness or intuition?

The doctor I work for says that a strong maternal attachment as a baby is largely why people are intuitive and empathetic.

In my first book of poetry, I thank my mother for giving me my story.

Do we make our stories, or do we walk into something that's been laid out for us?

"You've lost your innocence," my mother told me not long after I split from my husband. Her statement was accusatory the way she comes across when something is out of line with her thinking of how things are supposed to be. When I was innocent, I was not angry and when I was not angry we got along better or I talked about things that didn't involve feelings.

"You don't seem interested in the world anymore," my mother told me a year or so into my dating TWMIL.

"Are you alright?" my mother emailed me the other night. "You seem very down. If you need help, get it."

I used to think her concern was that I would die and she would feel responsible. I have come to think it is much more basic: she is overwhelmed by my huge emotions and so she tries to categorize them, name, and fix them. After my birth, she created a life for herself where emotions were less likely to appear. She had routine and safety and consistency. And near total isolation.

I was the grenade in her story, but I also didn't want to see my mother crumble. I cannot bear to see her cry.

Did you feel responsible for your mother when you were a child?

I felt responsible for my mother's emotional state.

I felt responsible for TWMIL's emotional state.

I felt responsible for my younger son's emotional state.

As though I was the manager of emotions for each of them.

Chapter Thirty-eight

I started going to the library again.

I don't browse the way we used to as a family; I look online and reserve the books at the library a few blocks from us, the one we used to walk to several times a week. I dart in and go to the reserve shelf, find my books, and check myself out. In the library system, my last name is the same as my children's.

According to my browsing history, I have checked out 423 books. This does not seem like a lot for a lifetime of parenting children and checking out all manner of things, *but you both had your own cards from an early age.*

We used to go to Barnes and Noble as a family. We spent hours sitting on the floor reading.

One night, early on after your father had moved out and you both were at his apartment, I went to pick up a magazine in which I was featured. It was the first time I had stepped inside Barnes and Noble since things had fallen apart. I was almost at the back of the store where the magazines were when I felt the floor rise up beneath me. I turned around and left and sobbed in the car.

I expected this same thing to happen when I first returned to the library, but it didn't, possibly because I am only there for a minute or two, or possibly because so much more time has passed, and I am hardened and medicated. I expected that library smell— the one that is a lighter cousin to the thrift store mix of musty pages and skin—to knock me over. It didn't.

I listed my going to the library as one of my achievements.

❦

Almost as delicious as clean sheets are chubby hummingbirds drinking from a newly filled feeder, the water clear, the red of the perch unadulterated by dust and dribbles. They sit squatty and independent. This kind of independence makes sense.

I make guacamole and egg toast.

I go to a yard sale and buy ten pink and red and purple crocheted coasters for three dollars. They look like flat flowers.

Fact: middle-aged, childless white women have the best yard sales.

My mother sees the coasters and asks if I am going to start entertaining. To her, this purchase is irrational. I have no furniture that needs protecting. I have no need for ten coasters, crocheted or otherwise.

"They are Frisbees for the mouse," I say.

I am developing a relationship with crocheted items.

I buy a dress that is part undershirt, part crochet frill. It is too short, so I wear cut off sweatpants under it. I feel true in these clothes.

I put goat cheese with honey on my toast.

I put Himalayan sea salt in my over-hard eggs. How to judge exactly the right amount? It's different than it is with regular salt. The crystals are so big they don't disperse. I did not know Himalayan sea salt existed before I met TWMIL.

"It seems that you like the drama," TWMIL said in one of many statements that made me wonder if he knew me at all.

"You're going to have to put out."

"I could have spent my time doing better things than replumbing your house."

Intimacies aren't meant for the page. You can tell your stories, just don't name names.

How do I trust myself when I am being told at every step that I am wrong?

How do I trust myself when my older son died on my watch?

I always chose family. Did I use family as an excuse?

To a childless white man, I did.

My father was a giant. Tall and thin, though his bones moved heavy. I am a bit like this, thin, but not gliding lightly through the world.

What makes bones heavy?

Worries? Inheritance? Palestine? Stories?

My story is both my own and the property of broken sisters across the globe.

For the brief period of time when I stood up and said *I want this for me because it feels good and I am happy,* most everything that mattered was taken from me.

I am learning alone.

I am learning boundaries.

Boundaries are different with white people.

Boundaries are different with men.

Close to a year After, I was talking with TWMIL about my younger son's reaction to his father getting remarried, how he had sobbed for hours. TWMIL mentioned child brides and arranged marriages and I said that this kind of commentary didn't help.

He persisted.

I went off.

I am tired of stereotypes and he is a white man, so he doesn't get to use that ticket, and besides, we were talking about my son's reaction, not TWMIL's opinion.

A Palestinian friend, an Armenian friend, and a Black friend all made similar comments and it didn't bother me, even as their comments also held judgment.

I felt like I was standing up for myself. By explaining for what felt like the thousandth time why he didn't have the right to make comments like that I felt like I was doing the right thing.

TWMIL shut down.

We rode our bikes home in silence and TWMIL closed himself in the back room, the one I had come to think of as my refuge. I pushed myself in, so tired of being shut out if I expressed something other than what was easy and expected.

He later referred to feeling threatened that night, that I had crossed a line.

White lines are so different.

White people need to declare themselves safe in boundaries made clear with Sharpies, cement, electrified lines. Closed doors.

One afternoon I drove to the next town to pick up donations for participants in a program I was running. The woman with the twelve cardboard boxes of craft items—five of them ostrich and emu eggs—got to chatting and told me about a book she had written on grain silos. She gave me a copy and when I left her house, I drove to a coffee shop that my GPS told me was nearby and I drank coffee on a leather couch in an airy room surrounded by white people while weirdly mesmerized by her lovely book.

A penis-looking pale bald man sat at a nearby table with his two children. His deep voice repeating his daughter's name (Chloe) sliced into the grain silo spell I was under.

Notice without judgment. Judge without censure. Censor.

Chloe's brother was complaining to their penis-dad. "She's never going to stop running her mouth."

Since this was a clearly repeated and mimicked directive, I disliked penis-dad even more.

"Stop acting like an elephant, Chloe."

Chloe was reliving a previous conversation. ". . . and I said Jesus Christ . . ."

Two women were sitting behind me talking about God. "There are some good Islamic people," one of them said.

Penis-father looked over at me.

I had a fling with a military man who had many of the superficial characteristics of penis-father. He was not someone I'd want to know in real life, but I slept with him and enjoyed it and once afterwards he stood up and said *Allahu akbar*, which was both horrifying and the most honest thing he could have said at that moment.

You fetishize each other, Thabet said about my attraction to white military men who I find exotic, dangerous, and vulnerable in equal measure.

"Shut up, please," said Chloe's brother. Penis-dad said nothing, glanced my way. Again.

All of the customers at the coffee shop were white. All of the employees were Latine. The border is less than an hour away. The temperature was in the triple digits.

Chloe and her brother and penis-dad got up to leave.

The two women behind me were talking about their relationship with God.

This is America.

Chloe's mother arrived. She was in uniform.

Penis-dad did not look my way again.

Some months later my younger son and I went for a drive and ended up at the same coffee shop. Everyone inside stared at him. "Do you want to sit outside?" he asked. It was a November afternoon in the eighties and we sat out on the porch and two groups of people stared at us. One woman walked by and smiled sweetly the way people used to when the boys were little, which tried to make up for the furtive, unsmiling glances of all of the other people.

After my son finished his sandwich, he asked if I wanted to walk while I drank my coffee. I forget the power ugly looks can carry. Where I think I can blend and play with expectations, he cannot and fundamentally takes the opposite approach, very this-is-me, take-it-or-leave-it.

We walked around the buildings that surrounded the coffee shop and crossed a street and sat on a bench in front of a pecan grove. We watched people driving by, mostly older and white with their mouths open, which reduced my younger son to giggles and hilarious imitations.

Something flew near us and then back toward a pecan tree. It was greenish gray and the size of a large hummingbird but flying like a bug, like a very thick, thick dragonfly. I followed where it went, even though it involved trespassing, but couldn't find it.

"That was some *Alice in Wonderland* shit right there," my younger son said.

When I first knew TWMIL, we would go on adventures in the desert. One time we drove up by a mine. He followed the perimeter of the fence and found a hole and even though it was clearly trespassing, and even though this was something I would not ever do normally, I entered without a second thought. There were interesting, rusted items lying about and I may or may not have picked up a metal object and taken it with me.

Another time we went for a hike and climbed a rock. I do not like heights, and I am not coordinated, but I went along with it, even when we climbed up a steep rock that was dozens of feet from the ground. Later he would say that he thought things were a bit dicey in that spot, that we could have fallen. It never crossed my mind that he wouldn't have been able to get us out of a situation we had gotten ourselves into.

"Women have such a skewed perception of what men can do," one of my supervisors once told me. "Like just because you are a man you are going to be able to fix a situation."

Well, yeah.

There is no wizard.

❧

We did it! *your ex-girlfriend told us you'd said when you had arrived at your first camping location on your two-week driving tour.* We did it! *I can hear your voice. I can see the deep satisfaction you must have felt. And every time I think this, my insides crumble a little.*

We did it! I tell myself in the car when I come out of the grocery store.

We did it! I tell myself when I've gotten through another day.

Learning to do a handstand builds body awareness through alignment and balance.

Max Shank says, "The handstand is perhaps the most honest expression of full-body integration—strength, mobility, and balance all coordinated together. This ability (full-body integration) is the keystone for total health and athleticism."

Mind, body, soul.

"Learn how to make the anchor point (and your center of gravity) strong and stable. Once you light up your core the RIGHT WAY, you'll be amazed at how strong everything becomes, and how much easier handstands are."

It is "freedom of expression in just one balance point."

Chapter Thirty-nine

Today is my best-friend-growing-up's fiftieth birthday. Our forty-seven-year-old sisterhood/friendship has been sealed away for almost four years.

My younger son is working.

TWMIL is "choosing happiness."

Raad is still dead.

I walk the 1.4 miles to the Poetry Center where Morgan Parker and Tommy Pico are giving a reading and I settle myself in the back of the room where I can see everything and no one can creep up behind me, as though this is a real concern. A South Asian girl walks toward her seat, trailed by a white boy who is telling her she just needs "to hang out and have fun."

What is it about white men and having fun?

A new pulse ripples through the room as the guests of honor arrive. Morgan wears flip-flops and jeans. Tommy's got on a tank top and will read from folded papers. They lean into each other and giggle, read each other's poems. Is this what it looks like to move through life with a closest friend? Who gives a shit if you wear flip-flops or a tank top?

The hour is up too quickly and the audience dissolves into clumps.

In spite of familiar faces, books for sale—I should buy *There are Things More Beautiful than Beyoncé* and tell Morgan that when I read "When A Man I Love Jerks Off in My Bed Next to Me and Falls Asleep" something in me woke up, that I added her to my pile of vitamin readings—in spite of the lost heartbeat these two magicians managed to find inside of me, I walk out into the night and head home.

It takes me thirty seconds to cross six lanes of traffic. That's five seconds a lane, which seems like a lot.

The smell of rotted death hangs over the northeast corner of Speedway and Campbell. A man approaches from my left. I fight the urge to vomit at both of these encroachments. One of my characters senses evil in people and the really bad ones make her puke. Perhaps another awful detail of my writing has come true.

Perhaps I wrote what was already there.

In parallel steps, he and I cross six more lanes. He is still on my left and could push me into traffic if he wanted, a possibility I spend all thirty seconds considering.

My younger son texts that he forgot to bring dinner with him to work, even though I reminded him twice, and could I please bring him some food. TWMIL would say to ignore him, that he has to learn, and while that is true, it also doesn't hurt to be kind.

I don't feel like getting in the car as soon as I get home. I want to stop here at this aluminum table in front of Miss Saigon and get spring rolls and peanut sauce.

My desire to be beholden to no one leaves me spending a lot of time alone.

I am drawn to TWMIL's moving location on our shared map that he hasn't turned off. I am a little obsessed by the fact that he still shops at REI, eats out most nights, takes trips, that nothing on his map has changed except visits to my house. As I walk home, I watch his tiny dot migrate away from the fancy Italian restaurant. Did he take one of the *yoga chicks* to dinner? Is he going home to fuck someone on the thousand-dollar mattress he bought to fit the king-sized bed frame he was so sure I'd love?

I wanted to love it.

I shouldn't care about any of these imaginings, especially since I am the one who spent more than a year pushing him away, who couldn't tend to another human's needs in the face of my own grief. I know it's not good for my mental health to watch this little dot head south . . .

Stop.

What I need to talk about is the skirt my mother insisted I buy when I did my first ever reading more than fifteen years ago. She said I needed to look *decent*, to show that I took things seriously because *dressing well* showed my audience that I respected them, as though a lifetime of laboring over stories wasn't enough. I was still married, pinned up by the thinkings of others, still responding to judgment. Instead of honoring my funky fresh self in jeans and some form of black T-shirt, giant earrings and lots of mascara, which is where I am most comfortable, I wore a long black skirt that would have been acceptable outerwear in Saudi Arabia.

I did not have the confidence then to trust myself.

Now, with life's bruises/lacerations/stab wounds/chemical warfare, I choose to tattoo my hands, wear what I want, break up with the man who loves me.

Walking alone and unafraid through the dark streets of my neighborhood, my mind wanders through my closet, piles up the for-other-people items.

The next morning, I spend an hour wrestling thoughts of death and dying before I manage to get out of bed. My wise voice scolds that I did not eat enough the night before—why didn't I get the spring rolls?—that I should do yoga, at least take the dog for a walk.

I do none of these things. I don't even stretch. Instead, I juggle words in my cool dark house with the dog stretched out on the leather couch given to me by a widow, TWMIL's friend. Not for the first time I wonder if in accepting items owned by people now gone I gave Death the key to my house.

The lift of the reading has worn off, occupies a hair's width in my medicated brain.

Raad is still dead.

Chapter Forty

I was running in the morning. Maybe it was Sunday; I can't keep things straight. I came to Country Club, no, Tucson Boulevard. A truck was coming. I ran. It was impulsive. I could have tripped and would have been flattened because the driver wouldn't have had time to stop. A yellow butterfly flew in front of my eyes—I could feel the flap across my face.

This is what you did. You misjudged and my world fell apart.

A while after we had split, I met TWMIL for a beer. We were sitting outside at a bar we had always enjoyed. I was cold and told him my jacket was in the car. I walked tipsy out of the bar and down the street when the lights went on for the train and the arm dropped just as I arrived at the tracks. I could see the train in the near distance. Without a thought I ducked under the arm and ran.

"I ducked under the arm," I told TWMIL when I got back, shocked by my own stupidity.

"I know, I saw you."

One night when we were still together, we were walking back from drinking somewhere. We crossed Sixth Street—at the same intersection where I would later see the man with the wooden water bottle, only going the other way. Just as we reached the middle of the street, TWMIL wrapped his arms around me and yanked me back. A car turned in front of me. I could feel the woosh.

Why was death always so close?

Don't get too caught up on the story.

It is Mother's Day.

I am still on meds.

I took a hit of weed at 3:00 a.m. when I couldn't sleep so I'm not feeling much of anything except a tiny zing when I come across a pair of men's boots on eBay *that you would love and for a split second I plan to send you the link before it hits me that this is the third Mother's Day without you and even though there's a darling green hummingbird at the feeder and even though I talked to TWMIL and it was okay, and even though your brother is doing well, it doesn't change the fact that you are gone, dead in your favorite pair of boots.*

My dinners of beer and popcorn are starting to catch up.

I am taking half a pill.

Woke up with my sweet dead son in my head crossing into something else. Or perhaps just ending. The birds tell me otherwise.

Two years ago, I was distraught. I walked through my days eviscerated. TWMIL got mad because I didn't want to go into the desert and collect wood for his stove.

"Live for the living," he told me. "It's about action, not words."

I failed on all counts.

I did not save my older son.

I could not live for the living, at least not for TWMIL.

Chapter Forty-one

I installed two security cameras.

No drug dealers or cops have come to the house, at least not in the range of the cameras. There have been plenty of delivery people, many new mailmen, our now-retired mailman, some solicitors, neighbors, friends, a baby javelina, one dog, two cats—one that comes regularly to drink from the water at the bottom of the gardenia's pot—a bird who flew in daily for a week (would tap at the front door and then sit on the arm of the chair), and a spider. It captured TWMIL when he came to drop off a birthday card. He squatted down and talked to Luna through the screen door.

More than anything, the security camera captures our comings and goings and my yardwork.

The first time it filmed me moving rocks around the backyard. I had gone in for water, seen that there were forty-six notifications, turned the camera off and then went back out. When I came back in a few hours later, I looked at the clips. There's me crossing the yard with a bucket of rocks. There's the dog following me. She watches intently and her ears flop.

I have never looked at myself from far away for more than a shutter's flash.

Narcissus looked at himself in the mirror and look what happened to him.

Instead of clearing all the clips when I would forget to turn off the camera, I started going through each one, then I started not turning off the cameras. I saw a slim woman, strong and healthy. Her hair was shiny and she had warm brown skin. She clearly loved her dog and her dog loved her. She was not efficient in her work—there were a lot of short trips from one side of the yard to the other, no economy of motion. She was not fast-moving either, most of the time.

The front camera captured a different set of routines.

My younger son and his girlfriend came in and out a lot, usually carrying food from a restaurant. After they broke up, my younger son went in and out of the front door, sometimes watching, sometimes pacing. He never looked relaxed. And then there was the woman again—me!—often with her dog. The dog would look up at her while she was unlocking the door. Sometimes the dog would put her nose behind the woman's knee and the woman would look down at the dog and sometimes say something and sometimes run a hand across her head. The woman carried a lot of bags to work. She went to the grocery store at least once a week. She carried many bags then too. Sometimes the young man would be waiting outside to help her. She walked with confidence and moved much more quickly than she did in the backyard. Her hair was shiny. Her shoulders broad and defined. She often went for an hour or two by herself in exercise clothes and when she came back her step was lighter. Sometimes the woman and her son would have funny conversations. The woman's voice was high with a whine to it.

Some months ago, I went to a coffee shop and saw a man who I thought I knew from when I was in college. I remember him as both odd and kind and that I had liked him very much. And then we parted ways and hadn't seen each other for thirty years. I was not completely sure it was him; when I had known him, he was skinny, a waif, who moved constantly; this man was large and bloated, and he moved slowly in the way of people with health or brain problems. Later, when I walked by his table, he said hello and asked if it was me. We greeted each other warmly and chatted a bit.

"I was sure that was you, but your voice is so much higher," he said. "It's gone up two octaves."

I mumbled about not smoking.

When I got home, I downloaded an app to train yourself to have a deeper voice.

This is how I relearn myself. I look from outside and create.

I have been told by patients and coworkers and strangers that they like my energy. I soak my knowledge from the security cameras with this good-energy person.

You are going to have to reinvent yourself.

Honor the whole knowing self, the one that wants to self-destruct after any contact with TWMIL. The one that had no idea Raad would never come home again and ordered a book for my mother off of Amazon while I waited for him, wide awake.

I am not losing my poetry; I am losing my shackles.

If I were a flower, TWMIL would have been the tree blocking my sun.

If I were a lion, he would have been a bigger lion.

If I were a deer, he'd have been a hunter who decided to care for me after he'd killed my family.

Dear Sertraline,

You swept up my brain, cleared the debris. You lifted me up off the kitchen floor, suctioned away my tears. You drove me to work, guided me through meetings, but where did you put my words? They've always been my secret weapon, my cache of coping, but now I sit dumb.

Yours truly.

Sertraline packed up my emotions before they made it to the gate, before I'd even had a chance to inspect them. It sealed them up in some deep dark strange room of the airport that officials would let you believe doesn't exist. It kept them there until a tired employee went off in need of a nap and found the room filled with unclaimed baggage. The free-for-all began. He opened every single suitcase not knowing he was about to shut the entire airport down due to suspicious activity, not knowing all of those fanciful things would be sent elsewhere—extraordinary rendition—for interrogation.

If I take half a pill, which half is it medicating?
Is that why I am better on half than whole?
My Arab half didn't need it but the American half does?
Or is it the reverse?

Chapter Forty-two

I was running for the first time in months and thinking how nice it was to be running for the first time in months.

And then I was lying face down in the street.

My hands had stopped my head from hitting. I looked up. A hawk feather lay arm's reach in front of me.

I reached for it and after a few seconds, I got up and kept walking. Blood dribbled down my knee.

The days passed. I was fuzzy and sad and irritated. I couldn't make sense of things. On Monday I went to work and one of the doctors I work with said it sounded like I had a concussion and that if I've had any head injury prior, I would be more susceptible to symptoms.

My neck still hurts.

A few weeks after I had met TWMIL, I was running backwards, and my foot caught a pothole. I fell and smacked the back of my head against the asphalt.

I was losing my job then.

Falling in love then.

Crashing my car then.

Watching one son become a man then.

Watching the other son lose himself then.

It seemed not unreasonable that I should smack my head.

My neck hurts to the point of nausea.

When my house is empty, I will do yoga.

When my house is empty, I will break.

Is this recent smack the final bookend for those five years in which I lost one son and nearly another, a best friend, a job, another job, two dogs, a bird, and in which I fell in and out of love?

Do significant events in one's life require bookends?

Helene, my beloved editor, visited years ago and gave me two light blue metal bookends in the shape of hands. I look at them every day and they bring me joy.

One holds between its fingers the ink print they took of Raad's hand at the mortuary.

It's just the body.

As a result of spending years trying to make sense of my 50.7/49.3, it used to be when I talked about anyone, I would explain their pedigree. I felt this was part of the story, that it was unfair not to include it, that I would be doing them a disservice. I was the opposite of *I don't see color.* I was *I see all shades of color and that's where I find the truth.*

I was projecting, as though everyone else had been denied their story too.

When I was first involved with TWMIL, his whiteness didn't bother me. He had quirky tendencies, but I adored the man underneath. I felt good that I had overcome my obsession with superficial details. I accepted him as he was.

I still do.

Chapter Forty-three

I have been off the medicine for three days. I feel like I have the flu. My younger son is asleep. The dog is on the couch.

I tried to play in the sandbox with white Americans and their pink skin and optimism, their tidy reality that names birds instead of recognizing them as ghosts.

Name-giving is an act of dominion.

I got lost in mockingbird MMA and was distracted by bird riots. I was awed by the hawks with their brutal messages and totally silenced by the sneaky owl ambassadors.

Everything was a metaphor. The baby bird in the garden trying to fly. His brother is dead a few feet away, has been dead a couple of days.

Our backyard is a graveyard.

The backyard is coming alive with ghosts.

The ghosts are blooming.

Gardens of memory in every corner.

I read a story about someone hanging bottles in trees to welcome ghosts. Or to send them away. I can't remember.

What if the exceptional ones are temporary? What if the birds are trapped spirits who know the truth and spend all day telling us, only we can't understand them and instead waste our time trying to classify them? What if sometimes they insist?

The weight of ghosts is measurable in memory, visible in birds.

I walk with my patient who died.

For the last week I have woken up to the buzz of the phone notifying me of action by the front security camera. Around 6:30, a bird flies under the archway, knocks on the door, and lands on the arm of the chair. It never occurred to me to go outside and let him in. Did I lose my chance?

The other night I was reading about alpacas and suddenly one of Raad's articles popped onto the screen without me having touched anything. How does that happen? How can that *not* be him at work behind the scenes?

I was working with a patient in infusion. There was a window behind him and a dove landed on the ledge, her beak filled with nesting materials. She looked in and I said *hello*, quietly. I don't think my patient noticed.

Coming home from work I see three hawks. They pull my thinking away from the swirl of stupid. Then there are six or seven and *I feel you close.*

I was in my lovely little office at work and the cleaning guy came in. He looked out the window and said at night he's seen an owl sitting on the corner of the building "right over there" he said, pointing to the next jutting-out section of this building. Just then a hummingbird flew up to the window. We are two floors up. I have been here two years and I have never seen a hummingbird by my window before. "Me neither," he said.

Shortly before I met TWMIL, I talked to a man online and agreed to meet him at the park. I had Luna and we circled the park. He asked to hold the leash. And then he let go when she pulled. And then he chased my dog across the park. And then he berated himself for the next leg of our walk. On the final loop, we neared the metal soccer goal that had been pulled off the field. An owl sat on the bar, only eight feet off the ground and maybe twenty yards from where we stood. I walked closer. The man hung back. I got within ten feet and stared at her, my dog by my side. The man seemed shaken by the sighting. We each separately googled the meaning of this when we got home and agreed it was not good. We did not see each other again.

After more than a year of me pushing him away, TWMIL and I went for a walk around the same park. The dog did not join us. As we looped around by the tennis courts, I looked up at the darkening sky and saw the silhouette of two owls on a light post. We watched them silently.

"I can't see you," I told him. "I can't be with you now. You are connected to every awful thing that has happened."

We watched the owls.
One flew away.
Joan Didion's got nothing on magical thinking.

Part Three

The sun rises even if all of the roosters have been shot.

—Unknown

Walk on air against your better judgment.

—Seamus Heaney

And what else can I do? Look after my teeth, listen to all the music I can, and keep going.

—Nuala O'Faolain

My phone flashes No Caller ID, hurtling me back to the unraveling years. Panic stirs up a rush of heart-work that thunders in my head.
No Caller ID was following up on the missing person report I filed.
No Caller ID was calling from rehab.
No Caller ID detained my (younger) son on the bus and could I please come down so they could release him to me.
No Caller ID flashed on a table in a bar, informed me that there had been an incident at a Circle K, and could I come down. "He's fine and he's not being held. He is a witness. Ma'am, this is a courtesy call." No Caller ID informed me that he was free to go.
No Caller ID wanted to know where my (younger) son was.
No Caller ID was calling from rehab.
No Caller ID said there had been an incident and subsequent questioning.
No Caller ID came to my door with two US Marshals *just to ask some questions.* I sent No Caller ID away *not answering your questions without my lawyer.*
No Caller ID called to explain.
No Caller ID wondered if I had any questions about next steps.
No Caller ID called to say he was doing much better.
No Caller ID came to my door and asked if I knew where my (older) son was even though they had just seen him in a thousand pieces across the highway.
No Caller ID has not called in a couple of years. Why now?
Voicemail pops up with a number from Pennsylvania.
No Caller ID is trying to give me a line of credit.
No Caller ID was the quarter that slammed my blood pinball-like all around my body.
For nothing.

Chapter Forty-four

I ordered seeds for organic Persian cucumbers.

Plant three to five seeds in each mound.

Some plants should be started indoors so they can establish themselves and then be replanted outside in a garden. Other plants (Persian cucumbers, for example) need to be planted directly into the ground and don't do well replanted because their root system can grow crooked.

I have planted several gardens with my sons over the years. We'd cordon off areas so the chickens and later the dogs wouldn't get in. Our fencing mostly came from found or repurposed items: stakes, coated wire, railroad ties. We bought bags of soil and compost and tilled them. We soaked it through and tilled some more. We made tiny indents in the soil and the three of us would squat down in the moist dirt and drop in the tiny seeds, Raad in his high-waisted shorts, tucked-in shirts, and rain boots, my younger son with his chubby face and fingers and wild hair. Carrots and radishes, tomatoes and sweet peas.

Our current garden area is completely constructed out of found objects, including two bunk bed ladders that serve as trellises. This garden is on the east side of our yard, whereas the previous ones were on the western side partly shaded by the mesquite trees. I tilled deeper and the whole bed sits several inches above the level of the yard. The walls are railroad ties TWMIL and I dragged out of a wash. I installed small sprinkler heads and a drip system, but I also water it twice a day for the first few days. In the fall we had a nice crop of chard. I just pulled up piles of beets and cooked them, but they had a sourness to them. The online advisors say to add borax to the beet trench, or to dig down a couple of feet and add kitchen compost a few months before planting. Next season.

I wrote a story about a gardener who visited another country and saw a magnificent tree. He stole a seedling and wrapped it up in a silk handkerchief and brought it back home with him. He planted it and cultivated and consulted experts and provided soil and sunlight and all sorts of fertilizers, but the tree grew oddly and did not ever look like the magnificent tree he had fallen in love with. For one thing, his tree stood crooked, no matter how he pruned and cleared the area around it. *Chueco.* The gardener could not understand this. He had done everything right! He had followed the instructions and listened to experts! He had let it grow freely!

Some plants need to grow directly in the soil and cannot be transplanted as they may suffer from transplant shock. If the root ball is exposed at all it will dry out and the plant will not thrive.

I bloomed and blossomed with a family, as a mother. I grew sprouts and buds and flowers and in the Terrible Years I've been sheared down to my very base, like the fig tree that half-died and now is growing leaves from the ground up. The light is different and all the nutrients I am getting are turning my sparse shoots yellow; they eventually wither and die. I will start over, this time with the good soil, the organic mulch. Clear all those trees that are blocking the sun. To be fair, I am planted in some very rich soil, so with a little help, I should be okay.

ॐ

Does being part of a theft count as childhood trauma?

Does being the theft itself make me an accessory?

Was it scribbled into my DNA from my parents' scrambled embraces that I am a thief or that I am in possession of stolen goods or that I am the missing masterpiece? Hahaha I am the Jordanian Mona Lisa, misplaced Vermeer, Abdul de Milo's stolen seed my covert mother carried in her uterus in the ultimate undercover operation.

A baby too-wanted carries power from places unseen.

A baby not-wanted carries fury from hell.

All of my unfortunate choices claimed me: *You're American.*

At one of my first readings, even though I was probably wearing the long black skirt, someone said, "Look how you dress! You don't look Arab." *You are not Other enough, so you can't be one of Them. You are like me. I know you.*

We thought you were Kashmiri, the Pakistani boys in college said.

You look just like your sister.

You are like a sister.

You remind me of my sister, the Pakistani man said smiling after he sold me my first new car from the same dealership where Raad would eventually work. *You have the same laugh.*

Where's Gucci? an American tourist asked me in slow, loud English on a Florence road.

If you can identify it, you have dominion.

And if you cannot identify it, then you cannot claim it.

Chapter Forty-five

It is coming up on Mother's Day.

I am a mother of two boys.

That will always be true.

That will never be true again.

I wore it like a badge.

I am sitting at my dining room table. My feet are resting on chairs. The dog is on the couch, resting, but not asleep. My younger son is getting ready for work. The blue metal ceiling fan that came with the house twenty years ago spins its magic with only an occasional complaint.

I wish my patients Happy Mother's Day.

"I don't know anything about you—do you have kids?" one asks.

"I do," I say and end the conversation before she can ask anything else.

"Do you have kids?" another asks.

"I do," I say and end the conversation.

"Are you a mother?" another asks.

"I am," I say and end the conversation.

When I went back to work a couple of months After, one of my patients, who was just a bit older than Raad but going through the nightmares of my younger son, asked me why I had been gone. I had not prepared for his question, answered him honestly, and immediately regretted it. He stumbled with a response.

A decade earlier, I had given a reading and answered someone's question about my family situation honestly. I saw faces pull back in rumpled confusion, could feel the distance that had suddenly developed between us. The too-muchness of my answer.

I am a mother, I want to say to my patients.

I want to share our sisterhood of motherhood.

I do have kids. Two. One twenty and the other would have been twenty-two, twenty-three, twenty-four, twenty-five . . .

Would have been?

I don't answer because to do so would change the dynamic of the relationship. For the ones with younger kids who struggle with motherhood, it would add a burden they did not bargain for and so I do what I do best: I warmly acknowledge and then deflect the conversation away from me.

While most people ask about family to make conversation or because they are genuinely curious, three women have asked me for this story out of selfishness. One knew what had happened but wanted details. Another wanted to hear the story beginning to end. And the most recent one wanted a handle on the brown boys hanging out on her street.

"Your neighborhood is really white," Tony said after silver-coating our roof.

My neighborhood is so white that I have come to think of my Jewish neighbors as People of Color.

The first week we lived here, a neighbor introduced himself to my husband and asked him where he was from. "Palestine," my husband answered. "How does it feel to come from a country that doesn't exist?" the man asked. Recently, I ran into this man and after we greeted each other he mused aloud, "I wonder why we've never connected."

I hide in plain sight in white. I think I am a camouflage master.

It is springtime and I am coming home from a morning walk. I need so much more exercise than what I am getting and yet I can't seem to make myself get the more exercise I need.

A neighbor is out with her dog. It goes without saying that my neighbor is white.

While I see her all the time, I don't know this neighbor at all. Sometimes we wave. Mostly we ignore each other.

Today we chat about the neighborhood, her job, the pandemic.

I applaud myself. Normally I say hello and keep walking. I don't want to engage. To engage is to be vulnerable. I am a pro at keeping people at arm's length, a master of real small talk. Today I linger because this woman is a neighbor and we are living in a pandemic and I miss connections and I want to be open to the world.

"I saw both your boys for the first time in ages yesterday," she says.

I say nothing.

My younger son was hanging out in front of the house with one of Raad's friends the day before. Raad has been dead for more than three years.

"So, are both your sons at the university?"

Maybe she is just curious. Maybe she can't tell brown people apart. Maybe she really wants to know what my kids are up to, this woman with whom I have had maybe two conversations in twenty years, who has never asked me a question about anything, and who has given us all the stink-eye on more than one occasion.

I want to believe she had just found a moment of humanity in our conversation—that maybe she, too, would normally not linger and talk—and that she is genuinely curious. I want to believe that this is the reason she is asking and not because she saw two brown boys in her neighborhood.

"You don't know," I say.

I steel myself. To answer her question honestly, I must slice myself open.

To answer her question will mean I might need to dive into my bed or Netflix for the rest of the day.

To answer her question will drain out of me what little life I have stocked up for today.

I tell her that my older son was killed in a car accident three years ago. I haven't finished this sentence and I am crying. She stares at me blankly with a similar expression on her face that my old boss had when I told him that our supervisor sexually harassed some of the young female employees, the same expression that the old white counselor had when I had asked him to help me with my family story, the same stunned silence as the audience, and the same blankness as my patient. My answer is too much for them and they are neither prepared nor equipped to deal.

She says she is sorry for my loss. She shakes her head.

I want to believe that my neighbor is offering kindness in the few words and conversation that follow.

I want to believe that when I come out of the alley a couple of days later and almost walk into her and greet her by name and she does not smile and just mutters hello it is because she is in her own world, struggling with her own thoughts.

As I write this, a dove jumps around on our back patio. She goes from the dog's water bowl to the bush to the lemon tree.

Breathe, Ma.

My heart is in my throat. I cannot breathe.

Chapter Forty-six

My five-thousand-piece jigsaw puzzle had extra pieces thrown in at the factory. I would not have been surprised if my DNA ratio came back as 51/52, just a little impossible.

I have never had a lot of space or good-quality furniture or extra money, so when I set to putting my puzzle together, I pulled out the rickety card table my mother brought from her parents' house before I was born and set to work.

When I met TWMIL, my frame had been solid; I had all four corners and all of the edges completed, even the hard sky ones. Beautiful clusters clung within the frame—employment, friendships, household, family, writing—and while mostly full, there was an empty space at the center where TWMIL's early pieces slid perfectly into place. Over time, as he brought more of his pieces into the mix, other mostly completed areas of my puzzle began arcing and popping out.

Job.

Brain health.

Car.

My younger son's section was huge so he could afford to lose a few tiny pieces.

The arcing and popping out was not cause and effect; it was life. It's all about balance, I told myself.

And then the cockatiel popped out, her piece carried away by the wind.

My husband and I had brought Najwa home for the boys one 'Eid a year or two after we had moved to Tucson. They both loved her, but Raad had a special affinity for birds and Najwa was effectively his. We clipped her wings and she took short flights around the house and hung out wherever he was. When he was sick, she would sit on his headboard and watch over him, periodically jumping down to sit on his chest or to play in his hair. He carried her around, took showers with her, did homework in her company. He would later tell me that Najwa had taught him unconditional love.

When TWMIL jam-crammed his yellow and green recreational plans into my puzzle, he held the door open too long, and out flew the gentle gray of our bird.

I stared at my crooked puzzle after my younger son and I spent hours walking around our neighborhood staring up at trees and looking for her. It would have been easy then to pull out the few pieces TWMIL had added, to rebuild the tiny corners that had pulled apart.

But I couldn't.

I could not break up with the man I had come to love over a lost bird and her metaphoric representation.

Even as I knew.

On many days it seemed like TWMIL's colorful bulk in the center pulled all the other pieces together, even as the colors were so much brighter that they were the first thing you noticed.

I did nothing.

My puzzle filled up with more colors and shapes. While some things came together, more were popping out at the edges and even in the middle. I'd pick them up and try to find a different spot for them somewhere else. Even though that's not how puzzles work.

And then one February, in the witching hour, a tornado hurtled through my life and took everything down.

I stood numb for hours, days, months, years, staring at the pieces of my beautiful puzzle scattered across the floor, the yard, the world. The card table was mangled beyond repair.

How could this have happened? Hadn't I been there the whole time? Hadn't I loved fully? Had I lost my vigilance?

After more days, weeks, months, years, of shock and misery, I began picking up a piece or two and dropping them into my pockets. Some of the pieces were easier to find than others—especially the bright, bulky ones. My pockets were bulging.

I cleared a space, sat down on the floor, and began to rebuild. Without the frame around them, the cluster of bright colored pieces looked ridiculous, glaring, ugly. I put them back in my pockets.

I went for walks and worked in the yard.

I nurtured my younger son. Took him away and held him close. And then stood back and watched him go.

I began working again.

I planted a garden and moved rocks and built my own table that was solid, heavy wood, and close to the ground. I brought it in the house and put my pieces on it. I emptied all my pockets and began piecing back the intricate sections of jobs and family, writing and health. Over weeks and months and years I worked on my puzzle.

Many, many times, I tried to find a place for those colorful pieces, especially that one bulky center piece that had seemed to hold everything in place before. No matter how I arranged and pushed, that center piece made it so none of the other pieces could fit.

I kept it in my pocket for months.

Years.

I still do.

Chapter Forty-seven

I have been off the meds for a couple of months now. I did an interview and answered my most difficult question *where are you from?* with the simplest answer: *I have a complicated story.* Full stop.

It was both amazing and obvious. And I felt nothing. No extra heartbeats at the question. No struggle to find the words for the answer, as though sertraline has permanently rerouted my emotions, paved over the shame.

There is an odd byproduct; rage spatters all which way, at people who have nothing to do with my story:

My friend's husband with his tiny tub of seven-dollar yogurt.

The driver of the Mercedes who drove fifty in the number one lane of a Los Angeles freeway.

My son who slept in my delicious clean bed while I was gone. Massive rage.

The blanket of antidepressants has lifted and my rage creatures are peeking out. There are several of them and they are ugly.

Perhaps I will name them.

Massimo. Ferduccia. Zigamo. My asshole self I will name Jilipollas.

It is snowing. Proper snow falling down. The curtain by my bed is open. Hummingbirds have come to feed and sit, squatty and sprinkled in snow.

The last time it snowed here the whole city came to a standstill. Schools were closed, roads were ridiculous. *Remember how we took the plastic slide from your playhouse and went to the park and you and your brother, along with many other neighborhood kids, sledded down the hill? It was joyful in the way of snow and children.*

You are here in the quiet white, in the fat hummingbird, in my heart, always.

Chapter Forty-eight

We will find out that my mother has a compression fracture.

"T-1, which is at the very bottom," she says.

When I Google this I find that T-1 is at the top and this will create another folder in my mental bank of concerns regarding my mother. For now, she hurts all the time. Getting up and down produces pants and whimpers. The pain has affected her digestion. She swears that the pain has nothing to do with her subsequent constipation, frustration, and weepiness, but it has her convinced that she has colon cancer.

This is day seven. She has finally seen a doctor, had an X-ray, been given a prescription for the pain, recommendations for heavy-duty laxatives, and seems more relaxed now that help is on the way.

The relax has not trickled down to me and I drive to CVS bursting with irritation, mostly at myself for being an adolescent in the face of my mother's distress, for allowing forever-ago emotions to surface and derail me. When I step out of the hustle of late afternoon traffic into the unusually quiet store, a large Black man in a red vest welcomes me with boom to his voice. I say hello, get one of three mini shopping carts and begin my tour of deserted aisles, pausing here and there to load up on supplements, laxatives, pain relievers, and juices. I head to the pharmacy to pick up her prescription.

Jason, the scruffy young blond man behind the counter, is telling the pharmacist that he is going to lunch after this. He takes a long gulp of his energy drink and takes his time coming my way, as though I am an inconvenience rather than a customer. I give my mother's name and date of birth and he asks me if I have questions about the medication. I say no and ask if he can ring up the rest of my stuff.

He looks at my cart and says, "That is a lot of things, but I can tell you how to save ten dollars when you go ring up at the front."

There is no other customer at the pharmacy and after I listen to him explain in the time it would have taken him to ring up half my items how I can save ten dollars today by committing to pay five dollars a month and after I say with forced calm that I am not interested, he tells me "the pharmacist will be right with you" and leaves before I have a chance to repeat that I do not need to see the pharmacist.

Ben comes out from behind the counter. He is bald and has a thick red beard and mustache. He smiles while he explains how to use the medicine and says that he hopes my mum feels better. She will later tell me that she likes Ben very much.

I push my little cart filled with laxatives and juices and pain relievers to the front of the store where there are no other customers and as I pile my things on the counter I say to Dwain, the cashier who had greeted me when I arrived, "They don't like to ring things up in pharmacy, do they?"

"It depends—sometimes when they are busy, no."

With all of the frustration of the last week/decade/lifetime, I say "There is no one in this store right now."

He has a silver-colored wedding ring and is breathing heavily. In a softer version of the boom his voice held earlier, he says, "It's all about the love," words that find the pause button I have been trying to access for days and smack the righteous adolescent clear out of me.

I will tell this story to my mother when I get back and she will laugh.

Chapter Forty-nine

To be denied your story is to know Palestine.

I wear her dresses and am told they are beautiful until I say whose tired fingers stitched them and then they become acts of war. Unexploded bombs waiting to happen.

In jeans *you look American.* As though American is a look that erases blood and eyes and stories.

You are with us or against us.

Like teenage boys, America has no nuance or sense of history. Buzzwords change the landscape. That's why words matter.

TWMIL told me *you think too much.* I told him *someone has to.*

He also said, *are you still talking?* when I'd be in the middle of a story he had grown tired of or because it brought up his own, one he had spent good work packing in a box and shoving under the house.

Trauma doesn't ask for passports.

Trauma seeks a soft bed.

Palestine twinkles in the distance. To know Palestine is to know heartbreak. And vice versa.

To know Palestine is to know resistance. And to occasionally wear glory.

Does Palestine recognize her son who swooned over polished mahogany and withered in the presence of loud relatives? She was not a good correspondent, but maybe she had her reasons. And how about her wounded boy who painted his body to cover the pain, who fell into the darker side of America's embrace?

It's like this with relatives. They can be fickle over small things. They can demand some kind of attention. Like God. *Treat me this way or you are not mine.* As though you get to choose what blood races around your body.

I told my boys early on, *do not change the plans of your life to tend to me. Promise me that.* But Palestine won't let go, especially of her sons. Her daughters go on to have their own, but her sons stay stuck on their mum. They never let go. Even if it torments them.

I am diluted so maybe my eyes see with a filter. My translation is solid, but my perspective is not.

Or vice versa.

My mother spoon-fed me a love story about my father, as though he had galloped into her life on one of her adored Arabians just for her and had not been dragging ropes tied to the clankety cans of his own family. And because their love ended prematurely, it lasted in their minds for decades.

My sweet mother got spoon-fed her own over-sweet promises of a woman's life.

In summer, the dark tights that the sun has painted on me laugh at the white jiggle of my upper thighs.

My truth arrives with the sun and yet all my glories carry the night.

"Your soul is full of light, despite your name," Rula texts me just before she leaves the country to see her dying mother. I worry that she is saying goodbye and I will never see her again.

Months after I met TWMIL, my growing-up best friend and her mum were at my house for dinner. We were watching TWMIL replace my kitchen door. My growing-up best friend, who was weeks away from being sealed off from my life for good, said, "I like him for you. He can handle a lot."

In that tiny sentence, I felt like she was saying goodbye, though I dismissed this thought as soon as it came to mind because it had seemed so irrational.

She was the one person I knew would always be around.

Chapter Fifty

There's a plop of twigs wedged down in the crotch of some branches of the prickly acacia tree just outside the back door. I had thought the nest was abandoned until I heard shrill little squawks and saw the two tiny, pointy heads popping up. The mum was a mockingbird or a thrasher, one of those lean indistinct gray birds that are interchangeable in my brain.

For days after that first sighting, I meant to tell my younger son about the babies.

One morning I walked across the yard and found one of the tiny baby birds dead, splayed out in its pink fleshiness.

The next morning there was silence.

The following morning, I heard squawks and heavy flaps.

There's the mum and the other baby!

It is early summer and I leave the windows and doors open at night to keep the house cool.

The ceiling fan with the rattan-looking woven blades that TWMIL installed over my bed hums quietly. A whisper. An exhaling.

Doves coo with no regard for chorus or unison.

A woodpecker is hammering.

A little bird squawks. Except for woodpeckers and doves, I cannot connect tweet with the bird it came from.

The act of naming animals shows lordship or dominion.

Car engines hum and groan from the next street over.

Whirr chirp twitter vroom hum . . . never silence.

I do the dishes from last night. A hummingbird fluffs himself up on a twig of the lemon tree just outside the kitchen window facing me.

You are here as I wash.

You are here as I listen.

You keep me company the whole time and the dishes become a joyous activity.

Look up, Ma, *your voice tells me at some point on my walk every morning.* There are all these birds on power lines and trees and walls and some look down at me. *I know you are close. You say hello through a butterfly who flits in front of me, or a hummingbird that buzzes, above, then hovers in front of me, then splits.*

Exhaustion washes over me even though it's only seven in the morning. I lean to the side and close my eyes.

Losing so much means you have to start over in places you don't realize you have to start over. Only after you've been walking up-hill in flip-flops does it hit you. Rebuild. From the ground up.

Chapter Fifty-one

For the first many weeks After, my brain was stuck in a loop of Raad's last hours on earth and would freeze on certain images: Raad calm and happy and saying goodbye before he left for the evening. Raad driving into the night. Raad pulling over. Raad standing by the highway in the night in the rain. Raad walking along the side of the highway with his hands in the air. The driver not paying attention heading right for him.

Now I avoid thinking about Raad's death and instead think about his life and his presence.

You need to walk yourself through what happened. Start to finish. Just the facts. And then let it go.

§⋅

He came home that night.

Before that.

My younger son had been in rehab for a few weeks.

It had rained off and on throughout the day. TWMIL and I went to the Re-Store to get something for a house he was working on and then to Barnes and Noble where I drank hot chocolate and worked on a story while he met with a man who would later become his close friend but then was an acquaintance. The man was in the military and had voted for Trump. He gave TWMIL a bottle of alcohol, tequila maybe, to thank him for having done something.

When we got home, Raad wasn't there. TWMIL and I went for a beer at the market—now closed—near our house. Raad texted that he was home and that he had gotten potatoes as I had requested. I told him at this point I didn't feel like cooking and why didn't he join us for dinner at the Chinese restaurant a few blocks away.

He said he was tired, that he was going out later and didn't really want to go out and eat. He said he had downloaded the movie *Doctor Strange* that TWMIL had asked for and we could watch it later if we felt like it.

TWMIL and I went to the Chinese restaurant. There was a large family near us with loud electronic devices and I wanted to leave. We ate sweet and sour soup, cashew chicken, and something else. I didn't eat much, and we brought all the leftovers for Raad.

When we got home, Raad was sitting at the dining room table reading Rick Perlstein's *The Invisible Bridge: The Fall of Nixon and the Rise of Reagan*, looking happy and relaxed. He was wearing black jeans, a thick black shirt with white specks sewn in, and the belt buckle I gave him for his eighteenth birthday. The bear. For family.

I sent TWMIL home. I had the startings of the cold Raad had had a few days earlier and I wanted to be alone.

Just before nine, Raad came into my room and said he was leaving to have a drink with his friend. Earlier in the day he had asked if I would cook for that friend and Layth and I said I would, delighted that he was finally wanting to bring people to the house again.

I reminded him again not to drink and drive. "Use Lyft. Call me."

"I know, Ma," he said.

He looked happy, handsome, relaxed.

"Do you want anything from the outside world?" my beautiful older son asked me as he stood in the doorway of my room.

I told him I was good. I told him to have fun.

"Are you sure? Last chance."

"I'm sure. Thank you."

"I love you, Ma."

"I love you too, habibi."

I went to sleep shortly after that.

At 1:30 there was a lot of noise, banging, and the light went on in the kitchen.

This was the third night in a row that I had woken up to banging around in the kitchen—though this night the noises were different—so where normally I would have said *alhamdillilah 'ala salama*, that night all I said was *really?*

Where on previous nights he had apologized or come in to chat, this time there was no response.

The light in the kitchen went off. The light in the living room went off, but instead of shuffling and noise in his room, the front door closed.

I was confused. After a minute or two I got up. His truck was not there. I texted him, asking if he had come home and left. He did not respond.

I wondered if someone else had come in. Who?

I never went back to sleep.

I figured he had gone to see a girl, though I wasn't completely sure he had been home. I texted again a couple of times. I was more irritated than worried. I couldn't understand why he didn't just answer. Twice I picked up the phone to call him but never did, thinking I needed to back off and give him some space.

An hour later he was dead.

I had no creeped-out feelings the way I did when my younger son was up to things.

I was wide awake.

I read.

I ordered a book for my mother from his Amazon account.

I cleaned the bathroom.

Turning off the light felt like goodbye.

I lost a marriage and sought out strength.

Strength is within, chickadee, no matter how much life fucks with you.

Without medicine I wanted to blame and divest; with medicine I accepted.

Acceptance, I often tell my patients, *is key to managing this awful thing that's happened.*

Does producing enough dopamine, whether naturally or pharmaceutically, offer the capacity to accept things as they are?

I feel sad today, lonely, angry, lost, heavy, hopeless. I slept, ate, hung out with my younger son and his girlfriend and still I imagine a bullet exploding my head, a thought I've not had in a while.

Stay glorious, sweet chickadee.

Chapter Fifty-two

It has been years/days/minutes since everything happened/un-happened. Time shifts like some stupid puzzle, a block that's no-where to be seen flips back with two fewer squares and where once I could line up those colors, settle them into their row, now every-thing is unplanned scattershot, a primary hodgepodge.

Death fucks with your timetable, promises you that nothing will ever make sense again even though it's been years now and the occasional day works out. It's yesterday they came to tell me. It's today that early-morning thudding around the kitchen. No amount of medicine or drink, yoga or sleep is going to make that right again, though time sands away the edges.

Time and gravity are like two brats that spend their day fuck-ing with me. One minute we're sitting on the couch chatting and the next I'm in my bed. One minute I am in my room listening to instructions for crow pose, the next I feel like my innards are coming out my ass.

It's all one big series of metaphors.

People of science and medicine will demand facts and proof and when you can't come up with any will diagnose you with anx-iety or depression, give you a script, and send you on your way.

When the DPS officers came to my house on that February afternoon, they asked me if I knew where my older son was. I said that I did not know and that he had gone out with a friend and then come home, or I thought he'd come home, and then he'd left. He had not responded to any of my texts.

"We found his vehicle," they told me. "Do you know if he loaned it to anyone?"

They seemed sure about this, that he had let someone borrow his truck. I didn't think that likely. My mind ticked through pos-sible scenarios. I wondered if he had hit someone and fled the scene. I was rapidly calculating what could be done about this but couldn't get past the nagging that he hadn't called. Later I would wonder why my first thought was that he had fled the scene of an accident. The only accident he was ever involved in—when he hit a bicyclist—he had called the insurance company immediately, then called me, and then insisted on driving the man to the hospital. He was someone who took responsibility.

That was as dark as my brain could go that gray February afternoon standing on my front porch with two very bulky officers.

"Had he been having any trouble lately?" one of them asked. "Seemed down?"

"Not at all." Again, this line of questioning was jagged, not lining up with the situation they had presented.

The two officers excused themselves and went to their two vehicles. TWMIL sat on the couch fiddling on his phone and I fussed, opened the curtains, paced.

"Sit down and relax," he told me. "Everything will be fine."

Later, when I would replay the twenty-four hours on either side of Raad's death over and over, looking at it from a million different angles, I would wonder if TWMIL knew. Had Raad called him? Had he followed him?

Of course, neither of those things happened. That is part of magical thinking.

Our brains are wired for stories.

"Everything is not fine," I replied with a poison tone I never used with TWMIL, as though some part of me already knew.

After twenty minutes the DPS officers returned.

This time they wanted to come in the house.

This time they asked me to sit down.

I sat on the couch and one of the officers stood while the other one sat on the leather bench in front of me, our knees a hand's distance away. TWMIL sat down on the couch to my right. Or my left. I can't remember.

My stomach is twisting and my heart is tight as I write this.

I cannot repeat this story.

I cannot relive this story.

As the seated DPS officer was talking, repeating the facts over and over and over while I screamed at him that he was wrong and TWMIL tried to hold me down and I was fighting him, trying to get him off me, a hummingbird flew up to the window. *I am all right, Ma. I am here.*

A month later when I met with Sergeant Blue at the McDonald's, he told me that he had wanted to wait to tell me until they were sure, but that *there had not been enough to identify him by.* The true meaning of these words cannot totally compute in my brain and is perhaps why I sometimes latch onto the CIA story.

A month later I would find the silver charm safe among the debris by the side of the road where Raad had breathed his last breath.

A month later I would see Johnny Cash played out in clouds.

Chapter Fifty-three

I dared masculinity and whiteness and its centuries of colonialism/colonization with my silly brown-girl pride. I carried my 49.3 percent as an antidote, my 100 percent as my power.

Some part of my consciousness knew that if I could handle that, I could handle anything.

If I have to ride the subway at night, I find the biggest, scariest man and ask him if I can stand next to him because I don't feel safe.

You thought you were white.

I couldn't see how I was seen and couldn't figure out why ease evaded me. Threaded through my every day was the awareness that I was missing a key component to belonging, that something connected to my father was always wrong.

Why are you so dark?

Where is your father? Does he have camels?

Fat. Arab. Slime. Girl. This underground awareness that I did not belong was confirmed as I got older and I insisted that I be given access to what was my right—my father, my culture—my relentlessness was squinted at and disapproved of.

I was a pit bull on the neck of a giraffe, gripped in an impossible quest.

Alice said that she had never seen such focus in a young person. I didn't have the facts.

I know what's best for you, my mother thought, as she kept my story buried in that black-and-white cardboard box in the hall closet.

I know what's best for you, my boyfriend thought, as he planned my days.

We don't know where your son is, the DPS officer told me, even though he had watched them scoop up his parts.

We aren't married because you have trust issues.

I don't trust.

I don't trust white.

White has not been honest with me. Ever.

It's not that they are white, TWMIL and my mother, it's that they expect me to be someone I am not capable of being and that expectation grows out of them being part of the majority and of projecting that on me.

Unmet expectations are some deadly shit.

Expectations are premature resentments.

I have chosen remote or incompatible men because they keep my true self safe. Or rather, my true self is not attainable by them.

I have chosen partners I am never truly vulnerable with. The little girl me, the writing me, the mother me, I kept her safe. At what cost?

Allow yourself to be small in the world and wander.

I don't have trust issues. There are people, sometimes people very close to me, who are not safe. I have let them into my house in spite of what I know. I don't have to hand over the keys to everything just because they are in my house.

I blamed my mother for keeping me from all of my family. I blamed her for doing what she wanted. I blamed her for owning my story. I blamed her for colonizing me. And yet, her doing those things was what she needed to do for her.

I have carried around other people's luggage for all these years, burdened by problems not my own. I got distracted by the contents, stifled by turtlenecks in summertime, hideous but practical sandals for the beach, pants many sizes too small squeezing at me, when really the whole time I could have just put down the damn suitcases and walked out the door in my beautiful Italian dress with the wooden buttons.

The myth of one's own superiority must be protected at all costs. TWMIL believed that hard work was everything, that if you strive for excellence, you will get there. He had no space for irrational deviance or skewed systems. Addiction did not make sense to him. Emotions gone wild were not welcome.

I sat back and handed the responsibility of my life to these people because I feared the truth of what I had been told all along: that I couldn't do a good enough job, that I would get it wrong. And then, on top of failing, I would have to face their disapproval.

Has my puzzle always been within someone else's framework?

I am enough.

Chapter Fifty-four

It's an in-bed-writing sort of morning, but Luna is barking nonstop. There must be a dog pooping in front of the house.

I reposition my brain and keep writing.

Luna's barking continues. She bounds into my room barking. Jumps on the bed, still barking.

I get up, follow her to the living room, and pull back the curtains just in time to see three dogs rounding the corner: one black, one white, one golden, all fat and healthy-looking and utterly joyous in their frolic.

The morning is misty in a way we rarely see here, a beach morning.

For a split second I see Heidi, Bella, and Mud following you.

You always said our dog could see ghosts.

Spirits settle into us.

This is one of the many things that no one tells you.

As if there is a Someone With The Information.

A child dying translates awful for the day-to-day things like missing and coping and holidays and doors opening. There's also the challenging part of a whole other spirit settling within you for a while. It's not an easy fit, like putting on a wetsuit after a shower or pulling a latex glove onto a sweaty hand.

Spirits cling to the walls, words, memories.

And then they stretch themselves to settle in.

What is the weight of a ghost?

You came to me in the morning in bird riots outside my window, the same window that looked out on your growing up, that was witness to almost two decades of your footsteps wandering around the backyard, flying leaves and clipping prickers, kicking the soccer ball against the garage wall, keeping the basketball away from your brother, reading in the hammock.

Do you remember our visit to Tucson that April in 1998? We drove straight from the airport and pulled up in front of the fixer-upper Meme had come across. The backyard was so bare she called it the *prison yard.* All dirt. Around the edges were a few trees—fake mandarin, kumquat, lemon, and African sumaq. We would go on to plant eighteen tombstone roses, three mesquites, an acacia, a grapefruit, an orange, and a pomegranate.

We planted everything together and their father did most of the watering while the boys made rivers in the dirt, kicked balls at the garage wall. I watched from the window as their father found what peace he could, carrying a hose to each new growth. He hated the desert. The brightness gave him headaches, so he'd wait until afternoon had tamped down the power of the sun—if not the heat—and go from plant to plant and tree to tree in one of his many unfortunate hats holding the hose and thinking about God knows what.

"I never have any free time now that my husband is home," my friend texts me from the tightly sewn cocoon of her family.

You came to me today on the words of a poet I discovered shortly before you died. You told me I should order her new book. After you died, I discovered it in your Amazon cart. Her ache is raw in the way your death has left me. How does one get through something so out of place and wrong?

For now, I hold you in the words.

Outside my window it is still only morning.

How has this happened?

Chapter Fifty-five

"There is a picture in there of when you were a model or something," says the exterminator of the powerful photo my cheating friend's sister took.

There are books in there with my name on the spines, I want to say. Instead, I say, "That was a long time ago."

"Don't sell yourself short," he says. "You are still a very attractive woman."

I want to tell him that all of his responses are wrong.

He is white and young and Southern and has the kind of body I like, solid and muscular but on the leaner side. His skin has a sheen to it that seems unnecessary in the cool of the morning and I wonder if he is ill or high.

He has spent too much time in my bedroom.

I am not attracted to him or scared of him, but I don't like him in my house.

A former student of mine joined us for what turned out to be Raad's last Thanksgiving dinner. After she found out what had happened, she told me how glad she was to have met him and that he was clearly someone who had been loved.

Another exercise I like to do with students is offer a short phrase, "I know," for example. Write whatever comes to mind and when that thought is done, write the phrase again. Keep going until nothing rises up in your mind.

I know that I gave all that I could give as a mother.

I know that I stretched myself to do my best by my children.

I know I put them first.

I know that I loved Raad totally.

And I know that he knew this.

Chapter Fifty-six

My name means *night*.

My first word was *light*.

Too much light comes in through the blue curtains in the dining room. I added two more curtain panels, but still it was very bright. I hung a shade outside and the light is perfect through this triple filtering. The long shadows across the butcher block table are reminders of a good life, a dining room where a family shared many meals, not just one woman sitting alone watching gritty European cop shows on her laptop and drinking strong, dark beer.

Toward the end of our time together, I went to a bar with TWMIL and was especially sad. Going to bars After often ended badly.

If I had been happy, we would have leaned into each other and watched people as we drank, talked about fun things, made plans. Instead, I sat across from him with my back to the room. A woman came over to take our order and TWMIL said "something strong and dark and delicious."

"You've got that right here from the looks of things," she said gesturing at me.

Until their father left, we as a family shared most every breakfast and dinner at this table that I painted a pale green and then a sweet light blue and then totally peeled off the surface so that it remains with blue legs and a butcher block top.

Sometimes their father would sit in the corner and grumble at the brightness. He darkened many days with his anger that for years I took responsibility for, as though I was the sun with its heat and brightness that annoyed him and gave him headaches.

All that time I could have hung a shade to dull the bright.

Or he could have. Instead, he simmered and simmered and simmered.

Right there is the spot where he boiled over and everything changed.

⁊⅌

Truth is in the quiet after the television is turned off. In Raad's voice whispering to look up during our morning walk and I do and there are all different sorts of birds on wires looking down at me.

Love is the texts my younger son sends me throughout the day checking on me, the hugs he gives the dog, the occasional forty dollars he sends to contribute to the household, the more than two years sober.

Life is my eighty-six-year-old mother sitting folded on her fifty-year-old pristine white couch remembering when she used to race turtles with her friend Polly when they were in fourth grade. At one point my mother had twenty-eight turtles.

Life is the man at the ticket booth when I went to see *American Woman* who carried airs of my older son in his cheery smile, the darkness of his skin that told of a recent elsewhere, and a name that was easily pronounceable in English, but not native to it. I paid $3.80 for a fix of tragedy so that I could feel my own.

Life is the twinge in my whole being that comes from more than just tripping and landing on pavement. The twinge that stretches back for the last five years, slams me into the ground from time to time.

Truth is in the paradox of space, the unhappiness I feel with people around countered by the need to have people around.

I am the illegitimate daughter of a white American woman who worked for the CIA and a Jordanian landowning man who was married with six children. While I learned these things in increments and did not get to the last piece until I was well into my twenties, I knew my shame and my power before birth.

I made up stories and wielded a big stick.

When I was in middle school, I learned that my parents were not married.

"You cannot tell anyone," my mother said.

Within half an hour, I had called William, a boy I liked in the way I always like boys with whom I am totally incompatible, and I told him everything.

My mother was horrified.

My mother had fallen far from the pinnacle of white privilege to the hell of brown. She walked through these doors willingly, unlocked them with her CIA commissioned lock-picks. There was no emergency exit. Sirens were wailing.

Learning my father's real last name—that my last name was not his last name—was gifted to me as a teenager when my mother worried that I would meet a brother or a cousin and fall in love and have children with disabilities. I am not joking; this was really the reason she told me.

While other children snuck pornography and drugs, I snuck into my mother's cardboard box of paperwork and looked at the black-and-white pictures of my father.

My mother processes emotions differently than I do. When I was young, I didn't understand that that was a thing. I thought I was supposed to think the same thoughts, carry the same beliefs, and function as she did. And that I was failing her if I did not.

I was raised by Dr. Spock and Mr. Rogers and Bruno Bettelheim. While I didn't have my very brown father present, I had several old white men by proxy who in their gentle guidance did not keep me from being mean to my mother; I hurt and had no allies or other modes of resistance.

I was mean to my mother even though I felt terrible afterwards, my behavior proving what I already knew, that I was wrong. A mistake. *Ghalta.*

I was being told that I was wonderful and the best daughter but at the same time I was being told that how I was and what I felt was wrong. Why would I want my father? Why would I feel scared and frustrated? Why would I be emotional?

Live for the living. Grieve like the Spartans.

Even as she rejoiced in having a child, even as she loved me and nurtured me, I presented challenges that needed to be analyzed because I was not like her.

Later she would tell me that Raad was going to be delayed because I spoke to him in two languages and yet he turned out to be one of the smartest humans she had known.

I resented my mother. A lot. Sometimes I still do, but mostly I see that she was doing her best and what has passed has passed.

I used to say this about my husband, that he was doing his best.

Until he put his hands around Raad's neck.

I don't want to get lost in resentment because it is a waste of time, but unless I say what it is that hurt me, it remains smoldering. I am pretty sure that sort of thing turns into cancer eventually.

Raad is dead more than three years.

He was hit by a semi while walking on the highway at 2:30 on a rainy February morning. We don't know why he was there, why he seemed to be crossing after the truck passed. Why he had his hands in the air. No one knows. No one will ever know.

He could have been trying to cross and misjudged.

He could have been crossing and the driver of the truck was not paying attention.

He could have been playing chicken.

He could have liked the woosh of vehicles and gotten too close.

He could have been following someone or something.

He could have been followed.

There was alcohol in his system, so he could have been impaired.

It was raining so he might not have seen clearly.

It could have been a combination of all of these things.

It might be something completely different.

The driver of the truck could have been lying about everything.

It might all have been made up. He may be working for a clandestine government agency at this very moment.

We will never know.

TWMIL thought he knew.

TWMIL was sure Raad did it on purpose. "We've all been there."

TWMIL went to Raad's work and announced that he had walked in front of a truck. This was not an accurate accounting of what had happened. TWMIL told all of his own friends the same thing.

The last time we were all together as a family was the twenty-four hours before we took my younger son to rehab. We had to drive him to Phoenix and make sure he didn't leave before his admission appointment time. We took the keys out of the doors and took turns keeping watch. He was high and did random strange things. He went outside to smoke with two of us watching to make sure he didn't hop the fence. I think that was the day he threw a rock through the window over the washing machine. I still have not repaired it.

He was high enough that he slept and the next morning we went to a diner with TWMIL. We were all weirdly cheerful, like we were just hanging out having breakfast. My younger son got in the truck and Raad came to say goodbye to me and then walked around to where his brother was sitting and wished him good luck. They hugged. They told each other *I love you*. They never saw each other again.

Three days before Raad was killed, I went to the wash on Tohono O'odham land with TWMIL and some of his white friends, including a woman who on the last day I would spend time with her would say the N-word repeatedly in a bar. I walked ahead and talked to the universe. Maybe because my younger son was safe in rehab, I finally had time to think about things other than mother-worries. I was not happy in life and not happy in my relationship. I talked this through with the sky and the land, and then I said to all the universe, *please take him from me.* I was referring to TWMIL. Just after I said this, TWMIL called me and said a great horned owl had swooped over me. He thought it was going to attack me. I took it as the universe had received my message. I felt immediate relief.

I was a coward.

I could not tell the man I loved and the man who loved me that things were not right even as we were both feeling it in different ways. I was not brave enough to say that we wanted and valued different things and those different wants and values were likely not going to change and maybe we should not go on together.

In the name of attachment and survival, instead of taking some kind of action, I was willing to accept something that no longer felt in sync. I was willing to stay, just as I had with their father until their father crossed a line.

I was a coward. I could not stand up for myself and say, "I deserve more than this." I could not unblur the lines between my children, myself, and my husband. I did not know how. My lines with my mother had never been clear. I thought that was just how you did things.

Attachment equaled survival.

Raad and I talked so many times about the struggles of being involved with white people, how the person could love you totally but miss acres of who you truly were. How to reconcile those two things?

I was scared of messing up and getting caught.

I was scared of being alone.

I was scared of throwing away a good thing.

I was scared of who I really was. I didn't believe in myself, and I also believed in myself completely.

I was not enough on my own.

I was too much.

On some core level I had bought the story that only a man could give me legitimacy. After I filed for divorce, I was so relieved that I could have sex again, it is no wonder I made poor choices.

"We've all been there," my friends say.

When I met TWMIL after my series of unfortunate choices, I thought I had gotten it right.

And I did. For a while.

And I didn't. Ever.

I said I didn't want to go to therapy earlier in life because I thought it involved too much focusing on the self, which, in my view of things, was so American. I eschewed yoga for much the same reason. And here I am. Every superior moment I have ever had has come back and beaten me and embraced me. And I have embraced it. Eventually.

I was mean to my mother when I was very young. I said horrible things to her, the worst of which was *you are not my real mother*. I said this with such conviction that I sometimes believed it. At the same time, I wanted her to like me and approve of me and want to keep me and so I was constantly reinventing ways for that to happen.

That is how I got here.

I took on all of my mother's thinking because I had no boundaries because if I had boundaries I would lose her during the barn dance and be completely alone in the wide world.

I held on.

I held on as my husband was angry.

I held on as I was unhappy.

I kept holding on until my children were threatened. And then I stood my tiny self in the middle of my middle-class white street, waving my big stick at drug dealers.

What I needed all along was a machete to hack through these damn tendrils and slice up the kidnapping drug dealers to bits.

It's as though I don't have a story without their stories.

My life is defined by the absence of men.

I was terrified of intimacy. I didn't know how it worked. It could drown you if you weren't careful and I discovered you could be intimate with anyone. To a point.

I didn't understand boundaries, so I took on my mother's fears as my own.

My borders were porous, so I carried everyone else's worries.

What if you were born yesterday? Could you see the day more clearly?

Looking back, I can see that I did my best. Sometimes I was a bit selfish, but I did my best. Not when I was a child though. Then I was pretty awful.

If only I had had the wisdom to say *let's have some pancakes* when Raad came home that night, maybe then he'd still be here.

If I hadn't texted him irritated after he left, maybe he would still be here.

If I had kicked my husband out the day my younger son said that he was rough with them instead of waiting several years until he wrapped his hands around Raad's neck on possibly the only occasion he ever talked back to his father.

If I had stood up to my mother and said we want to stay and live in California.

If I had stood up to my fearful self and said we can figure this out. *I am enough.*

The if-I-hads can fill a tub and they make no difference. The only thing is to say what was, see it clearly, and keep going.

Because all we have is what is.

Shortly after our first renter moved in, I glanced out my bedroom window and saw the light glow in the little window that faces the yard. That was always how I knew if Raad was home or not.

That renter smoked even though on the lease it says no smoking on the property and just like when Raad was there, I'd catch the occasional whiff and be irritated.

Initially I wasn't ready to rent it because I had too much going on with my kids and I couldn't add one more thing. After the accident, I was paralyzed. In movies you see parents who keep their dead children's rooms intact so they can go in and . . . well, they always sit on the end of the bed and hold a stuffed animal and look around sadly. I don't know if people do this in real life too, but since he had dismantled his room to move out and was only planning to stay in the garage temporarily, his things were all in boxes.

From where I sit right now, I see the side of the garage. I attached a piece of lattice so that you cannot see in from window to window. I have closed off the door from our yard to the garage. I don't want to interact with people. I want the quiet and the space of my home. If I were a very rich person, I would not rent it to anyone, though I would welcome visitors. Maybe not having excess money keeps us social.

We've now had several tenants. Each time one leaves I feel a twinge of sadness.

How can such a small building contain so much loss?

Chapter Fifty-seven

Within a week of Raad's death, I began driving Gloria with Luna riding shotgun. We would park behind the gym at the edge of the wash. We climbed down, the dog and I, and ran. I would yell and sob while Luna sniffed and ran back to check on me. There was no peace to be had in those days, save for the occasional gift from the universe: the giant brown suspenders, the driftwood in the shape of an old-style movie camera, the hummingbird that waited for me at the top of the creosote bush where I stretched.

We sold Gloria to Carolyn, who sent me a picture of her and Vincente Minnelli when he was a guest at a film festival while she was a theater student. He was the director of *The Bad and the Beautiful*, the movie for which Gloria Grahame—after whom the truck was named—won an Oscar for best supporting actress.

Carolyn and Raad share a birthday. They both love old movies and while they only met a couple of times, they liked each other.

The day she came to pick up Gloria, her roommate came with her. He was wearing suspenders.

Cereal for sleep.

Cereal for comfort.

I add Honey Nut Cheerios to my Raisin Bran and imagine we are having cereal together and talking about the day.

There are degrees to the weight of loss. This one, this thinking, is the stuff of sinking into the ocean while completely conscious, your hands tied so you can't do anything about the weights on your ankles.

In the beginning, this happened a hundred times a day.

Into the third year it happens several times a day only.

I read about parents who do things like start foundations as a way to honor their dead children. This is a lovely sentiment and I applaud those who have the means, resources, energy, and time. I sometimes think there is an expectation for something like this to happen, especially if you are in certain fields of employment.

The articles that give me solace are the ones that say *things are shit and I did my best through it and sometimes I fucked up and sometimes things were bleak and sometimes I couldn't handle my job or my friends or people.* It's not that I need permission to feel what I feel, but sometimes it's nice that someone recognizes how exhausting life can become. Imagine your normal self. Now imagine your normal self tethered to a box of boulders that you have to carry with you wherever you go. Your steps may be lighter for a few minutes, but they may not be.

Never in my life have I followed the proper trajectory so why would this be any different? TWMIL thought this would strengthen us, or that I would find solace in him. I didn't. Maybe it's a character flaw on my part or maybe this was just too much for Us to handle. It doesn't matter.

That is the other thing you never hear. None of this shit matters. You do your best. You give of yourself where you can. You show yourself compassion. You genuinely try and heal yourself or allow others to help you heal, but the rest doesn't matter.

I am the ink, blue and bruised, that pours onto the page.

I am the gold nib of this pen, stained but sturdy, beautiful even after all these years.

I am the hand that holds the pen, moves with the rhythm of words.

I am the body that holds itself up.

I am the ache in the knees and fingers.

I am this body, this soul, this breath, this smile.

I am the water that fills my glass.

I am the glass that holds the water.

I am the dining table with its worn wood painted blue, now peeled off but strong and standing and holding its own odd beauty.

I am the chairs around the table, soft, welcoming, a little rickety.

I am the floor that holds us up.

I am the walls of this house, thick, sturdy, and protective.

I am the street that runs proud in front of the house.

I am the birds above, the lizards scurrying around.

I am the occasional bunny that wanders around in the evening.

I am the calm in the day, the bright of the sky.

And in this way, habibi, we are always together.

I never submitted an obituary to the paper—I couldn't bring myself to write one.

There was no news of his accident in the papers or anywhere online, which means I can pretend more easily to myself that he is still alive.

If I were to write an obituary, this is what I might say:

There was or there wasn't, a brilliant young man who dreamed of changing the world. He is gone from us too soon, February 19, 2017 at the age of twenty-one, but he is always with us. Born in Los Angeles, raised in Tucson, with roots in Palestine and Jordan, Scotland and Morro Bay, this young man was an adored son, brother, grandson, friend, nephew, boyfriend, lover, cousin, film enthusiast, student, and journalist. Honor his memory with donations to the ACLU in his name or to the Loft Theater. When you watch a movie or see a bird that makes you smile, know he is with you.

Postscript

It is late August 2020. We've had the hottest year on record. At this writing, we've had twenty-six consecutive days over one hundred degrees (by October we will have had over a hundred days over a hundred, breaking all previous records). There is no brightness meter, but if there were, it would be at *blinding*. We've had only three inches of rain since January.

My younger son and I have been living together in pandemic isolation since March. He is two years sober from hard drugs and alcohol. He has turned twenty-one and is shaping himself into a solid young man, an extension of that wonderful young boy I raised. He has held down jobs, had a serious girlfriend, bought a truck, and offered his help around the house in all sorts of ways. He is a kind and funny human and these last months have been challenging but also wonderful. We often take drives in the afternoon, sometimes ending up at Dairy Queen for treats—a chocolate cappuccino Heath in chocolate ice cream Blizzard for me, something fruity and icy for him—park in the shade and talk while watching passing cars. He is getting ready to leave the state, to live a life of purpose without the heavy of past choices, and while this departure will be painful for me, my heart is full at the thought that he can move forward.

In spite of the heat, we walk most mornings, though Luna is showing signs of age and can only manage a short around-the-block stroll.

In my running days, I'd make sure to get up before six; now I wake up when I wake up and make sure I have at least two hours of writing before I venture out, sometimes not until eight or nine.

On the day before Chadwick Boseman will pass away from the cancer he's been carrying in his body for almost the same amount of time that Raad has been dead, I take Luna for a meandering walk down alleys. She wanders without a leash and starts to head back after we've checked out some hawk leavings under a cluster of pine trees. We walk side by side in the slow warm of the morning and she peps up when we get to our front path.

I let her inside, thank her for the walk, and set out for a run.

My knees are not interested.

I make it a few blocks and then veer down an alley with its gentler dirt surface. On the right at the end of the second alley stands a white brick house that has been under construction for months. It is tiny, but at least it has some shade, an awning in the front and in the back to shield it against the brutal brightness. The wall that surrounds the yard is four feet high and extra house things lean against it: black PVC pipes, a sink, a cane, and a window screen.

My eyes stop.

Leaning off the side of the window screen, a gray parrot is negotiating its next step.

"Hi," I say.

The parrot says nothing but looks up at me.

Years of visiting Tropical Kingdom with the boys, of talking with parrots, remaining calm against their strong talons, of carrying Najwa and Zaydan around the house . . . all of this sits inside me as I walk slowly toward him.

"Are you having an adventure?"

The parrot says nothing. He has a band on his ankle and his red tail feathers have been clipped.

I pick up a stick from the ground, squat down, and hold it toward him. "Step up," I say.

He stretches a pointy talon toward the stick and leans into it, pulls his other foot on for balance. He looks at me.

"Hi, lovely," I say.

"Okay," he says and leans his head forward for a scratch.

"Let's figure out where you came from, shall we?" I say and stand up.

He is balanced on the stick but looking wobbly.

"Here, step up." I hold my bare arm in front of him and he steps onto it.

I cross the road to a house where two men are putting up a fence. I lean in. "Good morning."

They stop what they are doing.

"I found this guy and I am wondering if maybe he belongs here."

They stare, smiling huge. "That's a parrot," one says.

"It is," I say, also smiling.

I think most anyone will agree that finding a parrot on your morning walk in the middle of a Southwestern city during a pandemic is pretty much the best thing that can happen.

"Wow. No. They have dogs, but they've been in this whole time."

"Okay, I'll keep looking."

They're both smiling. "He's yours now!" the one with glasses says.

I thank them and walk toward the next house, the one I've run by many times that has the pretty pool in the back. There is a little front gate and they used to have a dachshund. The parrot jumps off my arm and flies back across the street and lands at the bottom of a palm frond.

A woman in a yellow dress is coming out of another house.

"Excuse me," I call. "Did you lose a parrot?"

The woman signals that she can't hear me and comes closer. We both put our masks on. "I couldn't hear you over the AC. I thought you asked me if I lost a parrot."

"I did."

"I don't have a parrot." And then in a flash of realization her face lights up. "Oh! But they do." She points to the house with the little front gate and the pretty pool in the back.

"Okay, I'll go get him again and you let them know," I say.

I cross the street. The parrot looks at me and slides down the palm frond.

"Looks like it's time to go home," I say.

"Okay," he says and steps back onto my arm.

"I enjoyed meeting you," I tell him. "I'm glad we found your home."

"Okay," he says.

We cross the street as a very concerned woman comes rushing

outside. "Oh, Snoop!" she says and leans her forearm toward me. "Let's get you breakfast." Snoop steps onto her arm and she takes him away, offering a cursory thank you over her shoulder, and goes inside.

I continue on my walk.

On my return lap, with the sun behind me, clarity fills my heart: Raad was on this earth as a guardian. His time was limited because he was not of this world. He was wise at three because he carried wisdom of other lifetimes. He is now back in his true form and busy with behind-the-scenes work.

The human brain is wired for stories.

At the park, a tiny girl is up to her ankles in grass moist from just being watered. She has thick dark hair to her shoulders, and while I can't see her face, her joy fills the air as she travels away from her parents.

And there I am with my own sweet babies.

What was still is; it never was, and it always will be.

And all of these things are true.

Windows down, we loop beautiful Turri Road, where some years before Raad drove for the first time.

This bright springtime afternoon, my mum, my younger son, TWMIL, Layth, and I are in TWMIL's truck, releasing Raad's ashes in places he loved.

Like something out of *a Raad movie*, I hold my hand out the window and release impossibly small specks of what was once the body and bones and teeth of my firstborn son and watch them scatter into the air on Johnny Cash's voice singing Bruce Springsteen's words in "Further on up the Road."

November 9, 2016
Daily Wildcat
Column: A letter to the country I love
by Raad Zaghloul

As Theodore H. White noted in his account of the 1960 Kennedy-Nixon match-up, there was only one country up to that point that modeled its electoral system on that of the United States: Weimar Germany. That republic lasted little more than a dozen years before it got Adolf Hitler.

That is not to say that President Trump will be a Hitler analogue—even that is too harsh. But for the first time in our long and storied history, we have elected a demagogue with no respect for the very cornerstones upon which this country was built.

In the years to come, there will be postmortems. There will be finger-pointing. In the years to come, the New Deal and Great Society institutions, which represent the very best of who we can be, will be torn limb from limb. In the years to come, the hyper-partisanship, wealth inequality and racial resentment we deplored yesterday will balloon to dangerous levels. In the years to come, this country might not be the shining city on a hill my ancestors sought, believed in and continue to believe in.

But we did this.

Abraham Lincoln said, "If destruction be our lot, we must ourselves be its author and finisher . . . we must live through all time or die by suicide."

Perhaps the apocalypse is not nigh. It is easy to resort to hyperbole when a candy-colored madman takes over the country you love and revere. But if there is one man who is to be the author and finisher of our destruction, it is the rapacious, conniving, two-bit hustler that this country just elected.

There is only so much blame we can put on the various evils that beset us this election season. Cries of fury against Big Money and party elites will ring loud throughout the country, but they can only go so far. If we now or have ever achieved the greatness to which we lay claim, then surely we are more than the sum of our afflictions. Surely, in the face of clear and present evil, we would have the courage to resist those forces.

Surely, we would vote to protect our neighbors, of all creeds and colors. Surely, we would vote to protect our Muslim brothers and sisters, even if we worship differently. Surely, we would vote to protect our brothers and sisters in the LGBTQ community, even when we do not share the same sexual identity. Surely, we would vote to protect the millions of our neighbors who have been covered by the Affordable Care Act, which President-elect Trump has promised to repeal.

But we have not. Some pundits have described this election as a "primal scream." There is no bravery, no justice and no glory in voting for a racist, sexist, fraudulent huckster because he pays lip service to your problems.

Today—be shocked or be joyous.

Tomorrow, though—be vigilant. Soon, the Affordable Care Act will likely be overturned. In that event, millions will suffer.

Soon, untold numbers of immigrants will face deportation. Millions will suffer.

Soon, Muslims will face new levels of discrimination. Millions will suffer.

Soon, the advances made in recent decades, vis-a-vis abortion and same sex marriage, will be stamped out. Millions will suffer.

Who knows what will happen. We have elected a madman who openly praises the virtues of unpredictability. So all of this might happen. None of it might happen.

We were warned, though. From the gilded sepulchre of Trump Tower, our next president has made hideously clear his disrespect for the free press, a total ignorance of basic human decency and an overt repudiation of the democratic process.

Perhaps this is melodramatic. But I think not.

I am the son and great-grandson of immigrants. It can be easy to forget that people actually do see this country as a shining city on a hill, but my family, who left from the shores of Scotland and the tarmac of Jordan, never did.

I inherited that love, that optimism. We must never forget the genocides, the countless human rights abuses past and present. We must never forget that one of our greatest presidents signed an order interning more than a hundred thousand Japanese-American civilians, and that our Supreme Court upheld that order twice.

But this country has always survived by the dint of our ideals and the audacity to hold fast to those ideals even when faced with overwhelming odds.

Tuesday night, we forgot those ideals and we abandoned our posts. This tree of liberty, too often watered by the blood of patriots, is now in danger of falling over.

President-elect Trump represents the ills within us, the rampant materialism, greed and deliberate ignorance that soaks American society. His true evil, though, lies in his ability to cloak our decency, compassion and devotion.

Let us not wallow in darkness forever.

Acknowledgments

This book is an embroidery of memory, emotion, and fact. As such, threads overlap (or fray in the case of memory) and colors blend. I have told it all to the best of my recollection, except in the instances in which I have changed names or identifying characteristics to protect privacy.

Different versions of some passages or events in *The Weight of Ghosts* have appeared in *Turnpike Magazine, The Markaz Review, Mediterranean Poetry,* and *why an author writes to a guy holding a fish* (2Leaf Press). Thank you to those editors for taking on my work.

Thank you, Kate Gale, for your profound love of this book and for giving it a home I could trust, and to everyone on the Red Hen team for all your hard work and book respect. Helene Atwan, you have championed me from the day my path met yours. Gail Hochman, you have stuck with me and stood up for me.

Thank you to *The Weight of Ghosts'* first readers—Noreen Carver, Houri Berberian, Alice Elliott Dark—for your deeply thoughtful comments and helpful guidance, along with your belief that this story matters.

There is a virtual community of wonderful humans who have kept me afloat/upright/upside down/balanced with their stories, wisdoms, and guidance, including Max Shank, Trevor Noah, Kiran the Nomad.
 Adriene Mishler, Prasad Rangnekar, and Michelle Goldstein, your teachings have been integral to my healing and sanity.
 Elizabeth George, your mysteries brought Raad to term.
 Gabor Maté and David Sheff, you helped me through the worst of it.
 Jesmyn Ward, Terese Marie Mailhot, Anne Lamott, Zora Neale Hurston, Lucille Clifton, Tommy Orange, Rashid Hussein, your courage to speak about all the things with total honesty got through to me when I was most broken, helped me to heal.

To the poets, novelists, writers, and artists (so many of you are all those things) and supportive organizations:
 Joe Bolton, you changed my writing forever. I wish you were here to know that.

For the many years that you have supported and championed my writing, my deepest gratitude: Randa Jarrar, Rhody Downey, Alice Elliott Dark, Marianna Pegno, Mary Carroll-Hackett, Vikki Spritz, Houri Berberian, Robin Brande, Marwan Mahmoud, Naomi Shihab Nye, Ami Dalal, Laila Shawa, Khaled Mattawa, Pam Grammer, Jordan Elgrably and the *Markaz Review*, PEN, RAWI, American Writers Museum, Tucson Museum of Art, and the Fulbright Commission/Foundation.

To my village of lovelies: there are so many of you who have softened my life in ways you may or may not realize, through hugs, laughter, sweet texts, phone calls, shared meals, bags of plastic animals/pistachios/groceries, encouragement, good company, and invitations to stay in your homes. You are friends and colleagues and neighbors. You are sisters and acquaintances. You taught my sons, guided and friended them, championed and forgave them. All these generosities, small and large, past and present, have lifted me up and helped to carry me through. They continue to do so. There are more of you than I can name; many of you will find yourselves in the pages of *The Weight of Ghosts* and many more of you are behind the scenes. To all of you, I give my deepest gratitude and appreciation.

In the course of writing this book, I came to see more clearly the familial love that ripples through my mother's side; it is not warm and fuzzy but it is tenacious and firm. Did it begin with my grandfather as he worked his way out of Kensington? Or long before that in Glasgow? It flows through the generations, and I am grateful to have experienced it in many forms through Addy (Adrienne) Bachrach, Alice, and Robin Kirby. Mom, you have given me so much, done your best, kept me safe. You have been there for me always, supportive, forgiving, and accepting, even if I couldn't always see it. I fought you to claim my story and still you supported me; I am fairly certain that is the definition of love. I like to think that I passed this fierce love onto the boys, that on some level they know it in their bones. Rabiah, I stand in awe at what you have done for yourself, how much you have worked to heal, and how wise you have become in the process. Would that the weight of love from which you come hold you, support you, and help you to find joy in this very challenging life. I am so very proud of you, so very grateful for you.

Permissions

Biographical Note

Laila Halaby is the author of two novels, *Once in a Promised Land* (*Washington Post* top 100 works of fiction for 2007; Barnes and Noble Discover Great New Writers) and *West of the Jordan* (PEN Beyond Margins award–winner), as well as two collections of poetry, *why an author writes to a guy holding a fish* and *my name on his tongue*. Laila has two master's degrees (UCLA and LMU), was a Fulbright recipient, and currently lives in Tucson, Arizona, where she works as a counselor, museum educator, and creative writing teacher.